BADGER ASSEMBLY STORIES

CITIZENSHIP AND PSHE VOLUME II

Ages 5-7

Andy and Barbara Seed

Badger Publishing
15 Wedgwood Gate, Pin Green Industrial Estate, Stevenage, Hertfordshire SG1 4SU
Telephone: 01438 356907 Fax: 01438 747015

Cover photograph: Educational Solutions Ltd

Introduction

This book contains 25 assemblies for children aged 5-7, written specifically to resource the non-statutory guidelines for PSHE and Citizenship at Key Stage 1. Each assembly begins with an introduction and then a main presentation, usually given by the teacher. There are both interactive and non-interactive follow-up ideas and every assembly concludes with an optional reflection or prayer.

The assemblies use a wide range of stimulus material:

- Original stories
- Fiction: excerpts from children's books
- 'True life' stories: factual accounts of people's lives
- Factual accounts of events
- Mini drama sketches for children to perform, with play scripts
- Poems, mainly in the form of cautionary verse

Each assembly focuses on a single teaching requirement from the four strands of the PSHE and Citizenship guidelines, as listed in the contents and on the relevant assembly pages.

Follow-up

Each assembly presentation is followed by suggestions for interaction to involve the audience in the assembly and to reinforce learning.

Interactive follow-up activities include:

- Closed and open questions
- Active response, e.g. vote, hands up, thumbs up or down, giving scores
- Quizzes
- Use of volunteers to assist at the front
- Discussion

Non-interactive follow-up suggestions include: a summary of the story; points to think about; reflection and prayer.

Using the material

The assemblies in the book are designed to be used flexibly: it is intended that teachers select the most appropriate follow-up activities and questions from the range provided in order to meet the needs of the children present. The basic core presentation of each assembly may also be adapted to suit the school, of course, and may be used, for example, in circle time, as the basis for role-play or other drama, or for classroom discussion in Citizenship lessons.

Questions to stimulate a response from the children might include:

- What might it feel like to be in this situation?
- Have you experienced a situation like this in real life?
- Why did the characters do what they did?
- Were they right/wrong?

What makes a successful assembly?

Good preparation is essential, particularly if drama is involved. Other key pointers:

- Use of props or a visual focus (suggestions are included in the book; don't forget an OHP or data projector can be used if you can't find the object suggested).
- Relate the contents of the assembly to activities going on in the school or community.
- Interactivity: music, songs, drama or any kind of audience participation generates interest.

Use the story or presentation to make a single clear learning point, which can be reinforced in the reflection or prayer at the end of the assembly.

This collection builds on the popular Badger Assembly Stories with Citizenship and PSHE themes, Ages 5-7, volume 1 *by the same authors – available from Badger Publishing, ISBN 978-1-84424-229-0.*

Contents

1a Right and wrong: Doris Don't

Objective
To help children consider the importance of actions which are right and wrong.

PSHE/Citizenship links
1a: likes and dislikes, etc.

Props
None

Introduction
I hope you know the difference between right and wrong – it's really very important. Today's assembly is all about a little girl, younger than all of you, who learned the hard way about what is right and what is wrong.

Story: Doris Don't

Doris was three. Her mum had to keep a very close eye on her, as you'll see, because Doris didn't always do as she was told.

On Tuesday, Doris wanted to look at the photos on top of the bookcase in the dining room. She couldn't reach the pictures, so she climbed onto the bottom shelf of the bookcase. It wobbled.

"Doris, don't climb on the bookcase," said her mummy. "It might fall on you."

Doris didn't listen. She looked at the photos then went to get her drink from the kitchen. Doris heard her favourite TV programme starting in the living room, so she ran across the kitchen with her drink.

"Doris, don't run with your juice," said her mummy. "You might make a mess on the floor."

Doris didn't listen. She ran to the living room and sat down to watch TV. After watching her favourite programme, Doris was hungry. She went out into the garden and walked over to the strawberry patch.

"Doris, don't eat too many strawberries," said her mummy. "You might get a tummy ache."

Doris didn't listen. She ate lots and lots of strawberries. After eating the strawberries, Doris had sticky hands. She went into the bathroom to wash them and she turned the tap on full blast.

"Doris, don't turn the tap on too fast," said her mummy. "You might slip on the tiles if they get wet."

Doris didn't listen. She went to play with her dolls.

On Wednesday, Doris wanted to look at the photos on top of the bookcase in the dining room again. She climbed onto the bottom shelf of the bookcase. It wobbled again, then it fell on her with a bang. Doris had a cut on her head.

"Mummy, don't put that nasty cream on my cut," said Doris. "It stings."

Mummy didn't listen. She rubbed the cream all over the cut.

"Ouch!" said Doris.

Doris went to get her drink. She heard the doorbell go, so she ran across the kitchen with her juice to see who it was. The juice spilled all over the kitchen floor.

"Mummy, don't make me clean the floor," said Doris. "It's hard work."

Mummy didn't listen. She made Doris clean the whole kitchen floor.

"Ooooh..." groaned Doris.

After cleaning the kitchen floor, Doris was very hungry. She went out into the garden and walked over to the strawberry patch again. She ate all of the strawberries that were left. She had a nasty tummy ache and felt sick.

"Mummy, don't give me that yucky medicine," said Doris. "It tastes horrid."

Mummy didn't listen. She gave Doris the yucky medicine.

"Eeuurgh!" said Doris.

Doris had sticky hands again after eating all of the strawberries, so she went into the bathroom to wash them again. She turned the tap on full blast. Water went on the floor but Doris didn't notice. She slipped on the wet tiles and flew through the air. It was a shame for Doris that the toilet seat was up. She landed head first in the toilet with a splash.

"Mummy, don't wash my hair with that green shampoo," said Doris. "It makes my eyes red."

Mummy didn't listen. Lots of shampoo went in Doris' eyes and they were very red.

"Owww," said Doris.

On Thursday, Doris did do as she was told. She had a much, much better day.

INTERACTIVE FOLLOW-UP

Questions

1) What were the things that Doris did which she shouldn't have done?
(She climbed on a bookcase, ran with a drink, ate too many strawberries and turned the bathroom tap on too hard.)
2) How do we know that Doris shouldn't have done those things?
(Her mummy told her not to do them.)
3) What happened to Doris on Wednesday?
(The bookcase fell on her; she had to clean the kitchen floor; she got a tummy ache and she fell in the loo.)

Getting the message

1) Why did Doris do as she was told on Thursday?
2) Let's see if you know the difference between right and wrong. If I say something which is right, put your thumb up like this. If I say something which is wrong, put your thumb down like this.
    - Telling lies.
    - Doing what your teacher says.
    - Looking carefully before you cross the road.
    - Taking something that doesn't belong to you.
    - Shouting in class.
    - Looking after your pets carefully.
    - Being kind to everyone in school.

Non-interactive Follow-up

Summary

- Doris was a three year old girl who often didn't do as she was told.
- Doris climbed a bookcase even when told not to by her mum.
- She did other things she was told not to: she ran with a drink, ate too many strawberries and turned on the bathroom tap too hard.
- Each time, her mum gave her a good reason for not doing it.
- Doris did each thing again and suffered the consequences.
- The bookcase fell on her; she had to clean the kitchen floor; she got a tummy ache and she slipped and fell into the loo.

Something to think about

1) Responsible grown ups like parents and teachers tell us what to do because they know what's right and wrong.
2) We need to think carefully about doing what's right and not doing what's wrong – or we could get into trouble or get hurt.

Reflection

Try to do what is right all of the time. Sometimes, doing the right thing might seem unfair but it's still the right thing. If you go around doing what is wrong instead of what is right then people might not like you. Think hard about what you do.

Prayer

Lord God, help me to do and to say what is right. Help me to be kind and fair and to listen to the grown ups who know what is best for me. Help me to know when I am doing something wrong so that I don't do it again. Amen.

1b Sharing opinions: Sonny and the Rocket Boys

Objective
To help children learn the value of sharing opinions and explaining views on things that matter to them.

PSHE/Citizenship links
1b: explaining views.

Props
(Not essential): a picture of a real space rocket

Introduction
It's good to tell people about your ideas. Sometimes other people will like our ideas and sometimes they won't. They may even laugh at some of the things we say, but that shouldn't put us off telling other people what we think is important. Today's assembly is a true story about a boy who did just that: he told others about an idea he had – a truly extraordinary idea.

True Story: Sonny and the Rocket Boys

About fifty years ago, in America, there lived a boy called Sonny. That wasn't his real name but it's what everyone called him. Sonny's father was a coal miner. Every day, Sonny's father had to wear a helmet and travel in a metal cage deep underground where it was cold and wet and dangerous. Then he had to work hard for hours and hours, working the machines which dug out coal from the rocks deep down. When Sonny's father came home, he was dirty and tired and he had a terrible cough from breathing in coal dust. Coal mining is much safer now but, back then, it was a very tough job, full of risk.

Sonny didn't want to be a miner when he grew up. He didn't want to go underground like his dad. The trouble was that Sonny didn't know what he wanted to do instead. Nearly everyone in the town worked in the mine and there weren't any other jobs.

Then, one day, something happened which hit the news. It was on the TV and the radio and in the newspapers all over the world. Everyone was talking about it, even in Sonny's small town in the USA. The Russians had launched a rocket into space and put a machine up there called a satellite, to circle the Earth. Russia was a big country across the other side of the world from America and most Americans didn't like the Russians. They were very cross that Russia was winning the space race, as it was called, to build rockets and perhaps put the first astronaut into space.

One night, Sonny stayed out in his garden to see if he could see the Russian satellite, called Sputnik, as it flew high overhead, circling the world. He waited and waited for hours until, late into the night, he saw a tiny flashing streak of light, like a shooting star. Sputnik! It was an amazing sight and Sonny suddenly knew what he wanted to do: he wanted to be involved in the space race – he wanted to build rockets.

When Sonny told his friends at school, they laughed at him. "But you don't know any thing about rockets," they said. "None of us do." That was true, but it didn't put Sonny off his dream. He found some chemicals at home and put them in a tube and he tried to light it. It was a very dangerous thing to do. Sonny's first rocket didn't take off, but it exploded with a small bang and set his mother's garden fence on fire. From then on, Sonny knew that he would have to get help and be extra careful with chemicals. He was also in a lot of trouble with his mum!

Word soon got around about Sonny's first attempt at a rocket and lots of people laughed at him. But he didn't give up. He knew what he wanted to do and he told his friends about it again. Some of them agreed to help Sonny build a better rocket and they called themselves the Rocket Boys. They went to see some of the engineers who made things for the coal mine, friends of Sonny's father.

The engineers didn't know anything about rockets either, but they gave Sonny some strong metal tubing and told him which chemicals might work. Sonny made a pointed wooden nose cone for the top of his second rocket and some fins like little wings, like he'd seen on pictures of the big Russian rockets in the newspapers.

The Rocket Boys' second rocket didn't get very far. It only rose a few feet before it blew up with a mighty bang which made everyone in the town think that there had been a serious explosion at the mine. At least Sonny and his friends were at a safe distance and they didn't burn anyone's fence this time, but many people in the town, including Sonny's older brother Jim, made fun of him and his ideas.

But Sonny believed that he could do better. He asked his science teacher at school, Miss Riley, to help. She encouraged him and helped to find him a book about rockets. Then a boy called Quentin asked if he could join the Rocket Boys. Quentin was one of the cleverest boys in the whole school. "Your rocket didn't take off because it didn't have a nozzle," said Quentin. He seemed to know what he was talking about, so Sonny let him join the group. The mine engineers made a metal nozzle for Sonny's next rocket – it was shaped like a small funnel. Sonny used the money he'd earned from his paper round to buy some more chemicals to make rocket fuel. This time, the rocket shot up into the sky. The Rocket Boys cheered and whooped with joy.

Weeks and months passed, and Sonny and his gang made better and better rockets as they learned from their mistakes and read books and talked to people. The mining company let them use some land well away from the town so that no one would get hurt by a rocket landing on them. The Rocket Boys built a strong wooden cabin to hide behind during launches and they found out how to measure the height that their rockets flew up to in the sky.

People from the town began to come and watch the rockets as they whizzed up to over a thousand metres. A local newspaper reporter was amazed at what the teenagers were doing. Sonny entered the school science fair competition with his rockets and won. Then he won the state science fair and was sent on a long journey across America, where his project was voted the best in the whole of the country. By this time, the rockets were working brilliantly: shooting upwards at incredible speed to reach nearly 10,000 metres, which is higher than Mount Everest, the highest mountain in the world!

Sonny became well known and was offered a place at college. When the Rocket Boys left school, the group split up as they went their separate ways. But Sonny never gave up his dream of getting America into space – of beating the Russians – and, when he was older, he joined NASA – the American space agency – and he worked on the giant rockets that eventually took a man to the moon. He had done it!

INTERACTIVE FOLLOW-UP

Questions

1) Why did people in the town laugh at Sonny?
   (Because he was trying to build rockets when he didn't know how to and he burnt his mother's garden fence.)
2) Where did Sonny get help?
   (From friends and people at the mine, and from his teacher.)
3) What happened to Sonny in the end?
   (He built better and better rockets and won competitions with them, then he left school, went to college and eventually joined NASA, where he helped build the huge rockets that put astronauts into space.)

Getting the message

1) What can we learn from this true story? *(That we should not make fun of people's ideas when they tell us what they think; that saying what matters to you is important and valuable.)*
2) Sonny told other people about his idea to build rockets. He shared his views even when other people laughed at him. Let's see if you tell other people what you think about things. Put your hand up if you do these:
   - Join in discussions in the classroom.
   - Answer questions asked by your teacher.
   - Explain to other people what you're doing.
   - Listen carefully to what other people say.
   - Interrupt people who are talking.
   - Speak loud and clear so everyone in the room can hear you.

Learning more

What is an opinion? Do opinions matter?

Non-interactive Follow-up

Summary

- About 50 years ago, the Russians launched the first space satellite.
- A teenage boy in America saw it and decided that he wanted to build rockets; he didn't want to become a miner like his father.
- Sonny told people about his ideas but most laughed at him.
- His first attempt at a rocket was a disaster: he set the garden fence on fire.
- Some of his friends agreed to help him – they called themselves the Rocket Boys.
- The group got some help from engineers at the mine and from a science teacher.
- They built better and better rockets, which flew to over 10,000m.
- Sonny won several science fairs and people came to watch his rockets.
- Sonny left school, went to college and eventually joined NASA, working on the giant space rockets that took astronauts to the moon.

Reflection

Next time you're not sure about telling someone your ideas, remember the story of Sonny. He would never have become a rocket scientist if he hadn't told his friends about his ideas. When the Rocket Boys helped him, he became a big success. Try to share your views and ideas whenever you can.

Prayer

Lord God, thank you for people like Sonny, who share their thoughts and dreams even though people laugh at them. Help us to speak out and talk about the things that are important to us, and help us to listen to other people's ideas too. Amen.

1c Feelings: "The Rabbit-of-the-Dunes' Story"

Objective
To help children understand how to recognise, name and deal with feelings in a positive way.

PSHE/Citizenship links
1c: recognising, naming and dealing with feelings.

Props
None

Introduction
Today's assembly is a story about a rabbit who was feeling very sad. It's taken from a wonderful book called *The King of the Copper Mountains* by Paul Biegel. Listen to the story and think about the rabbit's feelings as he tells his tale.

Book extract: "The Rabbit-of-the-Dunes' Story" by Paul Biegel

King Mansolain was very, very old. He was so old that his heart was slowing down. His doctor went to find him a rare plant to make a special medicine. As he went on his long journey, he told animals to go to the king and tell him stories to keep him going until he got back. Here is one of the stories, told by a Rabbit called Mee, all about his older brother Fliz, who looked after him.

Early one morning, when the sun was just touching the tops of the dunes, Fliz shook me awake and said: "Come on! Today we're going to have a look at the Great Murmuring."

Now this was something we were not allowed to do because it is not suitable for rabbits, and anyhow much too far, or so our parents always told us. But my brother was so bold that I felt brave enough to go with him.

We sneaked out of our burrow, creeping stealthily under the bushes to the top of the hill. There on the crest of our dune we sat quietly for a while. The sun shone warmly on our backs and, in front of us, far off, we could hear the sound of the Great Murmuring.

"We have a long way to go, Mee," my brother told me. "Maybe we won't get home tonight, but we can easily sleep out somewhere." That sounded like a nice adventure to me.

"Look!" Fliz pointed. "We have to cross the valley and creep along by the bushes down there, then over that high dune."

We started off again, scrambling down to the valley. I still remember the seagulls that were flying about in front of us. "Bad, bad, bad!" they screamed. But one of them laughed loudly, and that was even worse.

It was late in the afternoon when we reached the top of the high dune. The sound of the Great Murmuring was much clearer now, but there were still more dunes ahead and the tall grass that grew on them prevented our seeing anything much.

"I daren't go any further," I told my brother. "The Great Murmuring might be something dangerous that will swallow us up. Let's go home."

My ears had drooped onto the back of my neck, but now my brother stroked them upright again. "Don't be scared," he said. "I'm here, aren't I? I want to know what the Great Murmuring is. We hear it all day long. I can't live and get married without even knowing what it looks like."

"Are you going to get married?" I asked and felt a little sad, for then he wouldn't be able to play with me any more.

"No, no, not really!" he said and hopped down a sandy path. I followed and we continued in this way for quite a time. It all looked so different from the ground around our burrow. Sharp thorns grew everywhere, and long, coarse grass, and from time to time we sank up to our middles in the sand.

A bit further on we had to climb again, but I was tired and the sun had already gone down. Fliz tried to push me along. I heard him panting as the sand sank away under his feet. The higher we went, the harder the wind blew: the grass whipped against my nose and my ears were blown so full of sharp sand that it made me cry. But Fliz pushed and pulled until we were both on top of the dune. There the Great Murmuring sounded loud, like the rumble of thunder, and I dared not look. But Fliz did, and I heard him say softly, "Brother Mee, Brother Mee, I see where the world ends. I see the great heaving plain that the sky bumps into and that swallows the sun. You must look!"

My brother put his forelegs around my neck and lifted my head. "Go on," he said. "Look!" And so I looked.

I saw the sea and the red sun setting in it. Then I began to tremble and wanted to go home to our warm burrow, for the great watery waste and the thundering surf crested with white foam is not for rabbits.

But Fliz, my brother, began to shout and dance. "I'm going down there!" he cried. "That's the place where the scales of the world lie, the big white ones we call shells."

"No, no!" I cried. "Stay here with me, Fliz. Don't go near the Great Murmuring!"

But he went forward, and poked his ears over the edge. "One big white one," he muttered. "A beautiful big white shell to take home to my bride."

"But you aren't going to get married, are you?" I called. "Don't leave me alone!"

My brother looked back once more. "Wait for me here," he said, and with a big jump disappeared down the steep sandy slope.

Mee cannot see his brother anywhere. He waits and waits until it is dark but Fliz does not come back. With tears in his eyes, and fearing that the waves have swept his brother away, Mee returns home alone.

The King thanks Mee for his story and suggests that perhaps Mee will find his brother one day, and so that night Mee went to bed full of hope.

[Extract from *The King of the Copper Mountains* by Paul Biegel, reproduced by permission of Strident Publishing.]

Interactive Follow-up

Questions

1) Why did Mee have tears in his eyes at the end?
(Because his brother Fliz had disappeared and left him behind by the sea.)
2) Why did Fliz want to see the Great Murmuring, and what was it?
(It was the sea, and Fliz wanted to see it because he was brave and curious, and also he wanted to collect a shell for his future wife.)
3) Why do you think that the rabbit told King Mansolain such a sad story?
(The story was important to Mee because he loved his brother and had such strong feelings of loss when Fliz was gone; also, it was helpful to Mee to tell other people his story and how he felt.)

Getting the message

1) How can it help you to tell someone about something sad that has happened to you?
(It is good to share feelings; other people may be able to help; it can feel like some of the sadness is taken away.)
2) The king helped Mee in two ways – what were they? *(1. By listening to his story; 2. By offering hope at the end that Fliz might return.)*
3) Here are some things you can do if you feel sad. Put your hand up if you think they're good:
   - Have a little cry.
   - Tell someone why you feel sad.
   - Try to ignore the feelings and think about something else.
   - Shout and stamp because it's not fair.
   - Think about something nice to cheer yourself up.

Learning more

1) Feelings can be good as well as bad: you can feel happy as well as sad, you can feel confident as well as feeling scared. What other feelings are there?
2) How can you help someone who's feeling sad or lonely or cross?

Non-interactive Follow-up

Summary

- Old King Mansolain needs stories to help his heart keep going.
- A rabbit called Mee calls at his castle to tell him a story.
- Mee and his brother Fliz set off from their home in the dunes.
- Fliz wanted to find out what the Great Murmuring was.
- They went on a long journey towards the noise.
- The Great Murmuring turned out to be the sea.
- Fliz wanted to get closer, to collect a shell, but Mee wanted to go home.
- Fliz set off down a steep bank but did not return; Mee went home alone, miserable.

Reflection

Everyone has feelings: some are nice to have and others are not nice to have at all. If you are feeling bad or sad about something, see if you can find someone to talk to about your feelings and help you feel better. It's good to share your feelings.

Prayer

Lord God, thank you that you made us able to have feelings. Thank you for feelings like joy, happiness and excitement. Please help us to talk about our feelings when they are not so good, like sadness or loneliness. Help us to learn to share our feelings and to help those who are feeling bad. Amen.

1d Recognising strengths: Walter Finds His Way

Objective

To help children think about themselves and recognise what they are good at.

PSHE/Citizenship links

1d: thinking about themselves.

Props

(Not essential): a DVD or video case of a well-known Disney animated film, or a large soft toy of a Disney character.

Introduction

Everybody's good at something. Some people are good at running, some are good at thinking, some are good at talking, some are good at making people laugh, some are good at painting, some are good at dancing and some are good at looking after animals. The list could go on forever. The trouble is that it takes some people a long while to find what they're really good at – like the boy in today's true story.

True story: Walter Finds His Way

Walter was a boy who grew up in America a long while ago in a time before your grandparents were born. His family were always moving around, trying to find work. They moved to a small farm which was owned by Walter's uncle, but the family just couldn't manage farming at all and so they moved again.

Walter went to lots of schools but he never did very well. One of his teachers wrote on a report that Walter was a slow child. Walter wasn't really slow, it's just that no one had ever noticed what he was good at. He was good at drawing but they never really did a lot of that in school in those days.

Walter moved again to Kansas City, a big town, where he made friends with another boy called Walter who took him to a movie theatre for the first time – a movie theatre is what Americans call a cinema. Walter loved seeing the funny silent movies and he went there as often as he could.

But soon the family moved again, to a huge city called Chicago. There, Walter went to secondary school, or high school as they called it, but as he grew up he couldn't decide what he wanted to do with his life. He left high school at 16 because he wanted to join the army but the army told him that he was too young. Instead, Walter joined the Red Cross, an ambulance service which helped wounded soldiers in the big war in Europe.

When the war finished, Walter got a job at a newspaper but he was fired, which means he lost his job, because the owners didn't like his ideas. At this point, when Walter was in his twenties, he realised what he wanted to do: become an artist. Drawing was the thing he was good at, after all. He managed to get a job making adverts for magazines but it was very boring – what he really wanted to do was to draw cartoons.

Walter couldn't get any work as a cartoonist where he lived, so he decided to move to Hollywood in California, where films were made. He had very little money and he didn't know anyone there. He went to all the film studios but they all turned him down. He decided he'd have a go at making his own films instead, and so he worked on an animated cartoon. People liked Walter's funny cartoons, even though they were black and white and had no sound, and so he began to draw more and he even hired other people to help him.

Walter became really successful when he added sound to his little animated films, and especially when he came up with a new cartoon character that audiences loved. The cartoon character was a little black mouse with big round ears. After that, Walter's film studio started to make colour films and longer ones about fairy tales, including *Snow White and the Seven Dwarfs*.

Eventually, Walter became a rich and famous man, all because he'd found what he was good at. People who knew him called him Walt, not Walter, and his surname was Disney. Walt Disney made some of the most famous cartoons and films ever. He and his artists invented characters like Mickey Mouse, Donald Duck and Goofy, and made some wonderful films such as *Pinocchio*, *Dumbo* and *Bambi*.

The Disney film studios still make animated films today, even though Walt is long gone. You've probably seen some of them – films like *Finding Nemo*, *Toy Story* and *The Incredibles*, for example. It's a good thing that Walt didn't listen to the people who told him he was no good at anything, wasn't it?

Interactive Follow-up

Questions

1) What was Walter good at? *(Drawing cartoons.)*
2) Why did Walter sometimes think he wasn't any good at anything?
(Because a teacher said he was slow, and he kept losing jobs.)
3) How did Walter become rich and famous?
(He used his talent for drawing and started the Disney Studios, making lots of successful cartoons and films.)

Getting the message

1) What can we learn from this story? *(Don't listen to people who tell you that you're no good; that it can take some people a long time to find out what they're good at; that working at what you're good at can bring enjoyment and other rewards.)*

2) What are you good at? Give these things one thumb up if you're quite good and two thumbs up if you're very good:
    - Drawing, like Walter
    - Running
    - Singing
    - Reading
    - Throwing and catching
    - Making things
    - Smiling
    - Listening

Learning more

Sometimes we need to do things that we're not very good at, because they're important. Things like keeping our bedrooms tidy is hard for some people but it's important. What other things should everyone try to do, even if they're not so good at it?

Non-interactive Follow-up

Summary

- Walter was a boy who grew up in America over 100 years ago.
- His family were always moving about, looking for work.
- One of Walter's teachers told him that he was slow.
- Walter was good at drawing but he tried lots of other jobs before he became an artist.
- He went to Hollywood to become a cartoonist but he had to make his own films.
- Walter became successful and started the Disney Studios.
- Walt Disney created characters like Mickey Mouse and made many famous animated films – he became rich and famous.

Something to think about

Can you learn to do something that you think you're not very good at?

Reflection

We can't all be good at everything – there are things that some of us do well and things that some of us don't do well. Think about the things you're good at and remember to try hard to learn the other things too. Maybe, one day, your dreams will come true, like Walt Disney's.

Prayer

Lord God, thank you that you made us all to be good at different things. Please help us to do the best we can with things we find hard and remind us of the things we are good at. Help us to help each other throughout the day. Amen.

1E Setting goals: The Hen Who Wouldn't Give Up

Objective
To show that sometimes determination is needed if we want to succeed at achieving the goals we set ourselves.

PSHE/Citizenship links
1e: how to set simple goals.

Props
a picture of a hen and/or some chicks, or half a dozen eggs

Introduction
Today's story comes from a wonderful book called *The Hen Who Wouldn't Give Up* by Jill Tomlinson. It is all about setting and achieving goals, which means thinking of something that you would really like to do and then deciding how you are actually going to get there. Some goals are small – like tidying your room, for example, or reading a book – and some might be really big, like becoming a famous footballer or dancer. The goal in this story is probably somewhere in the middle, and trying to achieve it gets someone into a lot of bother...

Book extract: *The Hen Who Wouldn't Give Up* by Jill Tomlinson

Hilda was a hen – a small, brown, speckled hen – and she lived on Biddick's Farm in a village called Little Dollop. Hilda was very excited. Her auntie had just hatched out five baby chicks. Hilda was dying to see them. The trouble was, her auntie lived in Much Wallop and that was five miles away. How was Hilda going to get there? It was too far to walk.

She sat in her favourite spot under the hedge and had a good think. Suddenly, Hilda perked up her head. Of course! She would have to get a lift! She squeezed through the hedge and hurried down the muddy lane from the farm.

"There'll be lots of cars and things on the main road," she said to herself. "I'll be in Much Wallop in no time. Won't Auntie be surprised to see me!" But, when Hilda reached the road, there was nothing in sight. "Perhaps I shall find something further on," she thought, and set off in the direction of Much Wallop.

She was in luck. Just around the corner, there was a row of cottages and parked in front of them was a big, green lorry thing. It was rather an odd box-like shape, with an open half-door at the back. Hilda hopped onto this and peered inside. She could not see very clearly, but it seemed to be full of torn packets and ashes and old tins. It smelled very nasty. *(Pause here and ask what the children think the lorry might be.)*

Still, this was no time to be fussy. Hilda hopped daintily down and settled on an old cornflake packet. There were a few cornflakes left in it. Hilda was very fond of cornflakes. She was just finishing the last one when she had a terrible shock. There was a great clanging and banging, and then a shower of horrible things was poured on top of her! She was battered and bumped by rotten apples and sticky baked-bean tins and spiky fish bones – ugh! – all sorts of unspeakable things. Hilda was too shocked to squawk. She thought she was going to be buried alive.

At last it stopped, but worse was to come. A voice shouted, "All right, Bill! Up she goes!" and the whole thing began to tip up. This helped at first, because all the rubbish rolled off Hilda and unburied her, but it went on tipping until all the rubbish was piled at the other end of the cart, with Hilda, fluttering and furious, tumbled on top of it. It was bad enough to have dustbins emptied on her head, but to be turned upside-down as well! It was too much.

Hilda spread her wings and fluttered to the open end of the cart, which was now facing up to the sky. Just as she got there, the whole thing began to swing down again. Hilda clung desperately to the tail-board as it plunged to earth. When it stopped, she hopped off and began to run. She did not stop running until she was safely back in the farm lane again. She was shaking all over.

"Oh dear," she clucked, collapsing into a sad little heap by the ditch. "Oh dear, dear!" When she had rested a little, Hilda shook the dust off her feathers and had a good wash in the ditch. She felt a lot better after that.

"Silly me!" she muttered to herself, as she pecked away at a patch of treacle on her tail. "I would choose a rubbish cart! Never mind. I'm going to see Auntie's chicks somehow. I'll try again tomorrow – on something cleaner!"

And brave little Hilda cocked her head and set off home to the farm.

[From *The Hen Who Wouldn't Give Up* by Jill Tomlinson. Text copyright © 1967 The Estate of Jill Tomlinson. Published by Egmont UK Ltd and used with permission.]

You'll be pleased to know that Hilda doesn't give up. She not only achieves her goal and gets to see her auntie's chicks after several more adventures, but ends up doing something very wonderful indeed. You'll have to read the rest of the story if you're interested.

Interactive Follow-up

Questions

1) What sort of creature was Hilda? *(A hen)*
2) At the start of the story, she set herself a goal. Can you remember what it was?
(To go to see her auntie's five new chicks.)
3) What was the very first thing that Hilda did, to set about achieving her goal?
(She sat down to have a think.)
4) What went wrong with Hilda's plan to get a lift?
(First she couldn't find anyone to give her a lift and then she ended up travelling in a dustcart, and nearly getting buried with smelly rubbish.)
5) Did this put Hilda off trying to achieve her goal?
(No, but she decided she needed a different plan.)

Getting the message

Let's have a think about the sorts of goals you can set for yourselves today. It's not safe to plan to go on a journey on your own like Hilda did, so try to think of a small goal you can set yourself today at school. Listen to these suggestions and then see if you'd like to have a go at one of them.

You could:

- aim to be kind to someone who looks lonely at playtime;
- try to listen really carefully to what your teacher tells you ALL day;
- aim to finish all of your work by the end of the lesson, instead of wasting time chatting;
- make a new friend.

Put your hand up if you fancy setting one of those as a goal for yourself today. Or perhaps you've got another idea for a goal you'd like to set for yourself that you'd like to tell us all about? *(Ask a few children which one they will set themselves.)*

Learning more

Now, let's say that my goal is to be kind to someone who looks lonely at playtime. How could I do that? Settle down and have a bit of a think, just like Hilda did. *[Mime a chicken fluffing its feathers and ask for suggestions (e.g. Take a friend with you, if you're feeling a bit shy; think of something you can chat about or a game you can invite them to play, etc).]* Remember that it's always easier to achieve any goal if you have some sort of idea or plan to follow.

NON-INTERACTIVE FOLLOW-UP

Summary

- Hilda the hen has heard that her auntie has hatched five new chicks.
- She sets herself the goal of going to see them, although they are in a village several miles away.
- She settles down to have a think and comes up with a plan.
- She tries to get a lift in a dustcart, but gets covered in smelly rubbish.
- She escapes from the dustcart and decides to go home again.
- She doesn't give up the idea of visiting her auntie's chicks, however, and plans to have another go at achieving her goal the next day.

Reflection

Sometimes it's hard to stick at something, when things get difficult. If you find yourself just about to give up on something you set out to do, have a think back to why you wanted to do it in the first place. That often reminds you of why it's important to you and helps you to stick with your plan.

Prayer

Lord God, thank you that we have the chance to achieve all sorts of things. Please help us all to set ourselves good goals and also help us to achieve them. Help us to be like Hilda and not to give up. Amen.

2A TAKING PART IN DISCUSSIONS: BORING, BORING!

Objective
To help children recognise the value of taking part in discussions in the classroom.

PSHE/Citizenship links
2a: taking part in discussions.

Props
None

Introduction
Have you ever joined in a discussion in the classroom? A discussion is when everyone gets the chance to talk about something and to listen to each other. Some people like to say a lot and others keep very quiet. Here's a story about a boy who didn't like discussions.

STORY: BORING, BORING!

"Boring, boring, boring!" said Naz for the fourth time that morning. He was sitting in his classroom in Fulbrooke Infants School, complaining to his friend Michelle. Their teacher, Mrs Ravensworth, had just announced that tomorrow the class was going to have an important discussion.

"We're always having discussions," he said. "And they're never about football."

Michelle laughed. "Football is all you ever think about, Naz. Discussions are good – we all have a chance to say what we think. Anyway, the discussion might be about football."

"Oh yeah," said Naz, and flopped his head down onto his hands, waiting for the playtime bell.

When the bell went, Naz sat up straight so that he would be let out to play. He raced into the playground, having picked up his ball on the way out. He booted it into the air and shouted after his friends to come and play.

The children who liked playing football at Fulbrooke were very lucky because they had their own special area of playground to play in, away from the rest.

About ten boys and three girls came over to Naz and they picked teams. Naz always picked first because it was his ball and he was the best at football. Some of the others thought it was unfair but nobody dared complain. Naz picked three boys then Michelle, who had come to join in.

"What about goals?" she said.

"We'll have to use coats," said Naz, throwing his down onto the muddy ground. Another boy placed his nearby to make one goal.

Michelle kept hers on, feeling a sharp February breeze turning her ears pink. "It's too cold today." Naz looked around.

"My mum said I have to keep mine on because I have a runny nose," sniffed another boy.

"What about you, Hua?" Naz looked at a small boy wearing a smart denim jacket.

He shook his head. "I'm not to get it dirty – it's new."

Naz was getting cross. "Oh, come on, we've only got one goal and we're wasting footy time. We need two!" But no one else wanted to take off their coat, it was just too cold. In the end, they just took turns taking penalties instead of playing a match.

"That was boring," said Naz, as the bell rang for the end of playtime. He picked up his black coat, which was now covered in mucky footprints where people had trodden on it, and trudged inside.

The next morning, Naz woke up feeling weary. His mum looked at him sniffing with a tissue and said, "It looks like you're getting a cold. How do you feel?"

"Oh, I'm not too bad," said Naz, wiping his nose with his hand.

Naz's mum passed him a tissue. "I hope you've been wearing your coat at school."

"I always go out with my coat," said Naz, looking a little guilty.

"Well, I'm wondering whether we should keep you at home today. What do you think?"

Naz was just about to say, "I'm alright", when he remembered that Mrs Ravensworth was going to have a discussion in the classroom. Even though he wanted to play football with his friends, he definitely didn't want to sit through a boring discussion. "Actually, I do feel a bit funny, Mum. Perhaps I'd better stay in bed today." Naz pulled his best groggy face and lay down. His mum looked a little doubtful, but she agreed and went to get him a hot drink.

A day later, Naz still had a runny nose and felt tired, but he was desperate to get back to school and play football at playtime. Staying at home in bed had been boring – really boring. His mum wouldn't let him do anything except read and watch a bit of TV. He got up, had a shower and told her that he felt better and wanted to go back to school.

"Well, alright, if you're sure," she said.

At school that morning, a group of three boys came rushing towards Naz to ask him where he had been. He explained about having a cold. They moaned and said something about netball then ran off. Naz didn't really understand what they meant. Then Michelle came over and told Naz about the discussion.

"You should have been here yesterday, Naz. The discussion **was** about football – well, sort of. Mrs Ravensworth said that an old lady who used to teach at this school had died a few months ago. She left some money for each class to choose something for playtime. That's what the discussion was about – we got £150 to spend on equipment."

"Excellent!" said Naz. "We should get some new goals for football – proper ones."

"That's what most of the boys wanted, and me too, but Mrs Ravensworth wrote all the ideas on the board. There were loads: climbing frames, tyre swings, a trampoline, a play house, netball posts and stuff like that. Then we had a vote for the one most people wanted, although the trampoline wasn't allowed."

"What's a vote?" said Naz.

"You know, where you put up your hand to choose the one you want?"

"So, what happened?"

Michelle looked glum. "Well, the football goals and the netball posts got nine votes each – it was a draw. Mrs Ravensworth tossed a coin and the netball posts won."

Naz stamped his foot. "But that's not fair: I didn't get a vote!"

"Well, you weren't there," said Michelle. "You said discussions were boring, remember."

"But, but... netball – that's even more boring!"

"Well, most people don't think so or it wouldn't have won. I think next time you'd better join in the discussion!" But all Naz could do was sneeze.

Interactive Follow-up

Questions

1) What was the discussion in Mrs Ravensworth's class about?
   (How to spend some money they had been given for playground equipment.)
2) Why wasn't Naz in school for the discussion?
   (He had a runny nose or a cold and decided to stay at home because he thought discussions were boring.)
3) What was decided at the discussion?
   (The class voted to buy netball posts with the money.)

Getting the message

1) What can we learn from this story? *(That sometimes discussions are important; that it's good to join in; that you shouldn't judge something before it's happened.)*
2) We can't have a discussion with this many people in the hall but we can have a vote. Let's vote about the story, about what Naz should do. First, listen to this list:
   - Naz should carry on saying discussions are boring.
   - Naz should join in the next discussion.
   - Naz should not join in the next discussion.

   (Read the list again and ask the children to vote.)

Learning more

Why is voting a fair way to decide things?

Non-interactive Follow-up

Summary

- Naz thought that school discussions were boring.
- At playtime, Naz and his friends couldn't play football because they had no goals.
- Naz had a runny nose the next day and used it as an excuse to stay at home to miss the discussion.
- The next day, he returned to school but Michelle told him some bad news.
- The children in Naz's class had discussed how to spend £150 on playground equipment.
- They voted for netball posts because Naz wasn't there to vote for new goals.

Reflection

Try and join in discussions whenever you can. Try to listen to others as well as talk. Think about what other people say before you say what you think. It's also important to be patient when you put up your hand.

Prayer

Lord God, thank you that you gave us brains to think and mouths to speak. Thank you that we can learn to discuss questions in school and learn from each other as we listen. Help us to join in discussions and to think hard about the things we say. Amen.

2B TAKING PART IN DEBATE: HOW A DEBATE WORKS

Objective

To help children understand what a debate is and why they are important.

PSHE/Citizenship links

2b: taking part in a simple debate about topical issues.

Preparation

This assembly is in the form of a simple mini-drama with a play script. You will need five children to read the parts: each must be a good, confident reader with a clear voice. You will need to have a couple of practices with these children and each will need a copy of the script. The 'debate' is highly simplified.

Introduction

How do people who run our country decide what to do? How do they know what people think about things? What happens if some of them disagree? Well, one of the ways they decide what to do is by having something called a debate. What is a debate and how does it work? Well, we're going to have one right now so you can see!

DRAMA SCRIPT: HOW A DEBATE WORKS

Teacher: Today's debate is about housing. Who has a proposal or suggestion to make?

Child A: I do. My suggestion is that lots of new houses should be built in our country.

Teacher: Thank you. Now, who is going to speak in favour of this proposal?

Child B: I am. I support the idea of building lots of new houses in this country. I think it's a good idea for three reasons. First, it will give homeless people somewhere to live. Second, houses are very expensive at the moment. Many young people cannot afford to buy a house to live in. Some of the new houses can be built at a low cost for these people. The third reason why I think this is a good idea is that building lots of houses will give lots of people jobs and help them to earn money.

Teacher: Thank you. Is there anyone else who supports this suggestion?

Child C: I support the idea of building new houses because I know lots of people who live in dirty, damp old houses and flats which are not good places to live. If new houses were built then these horrible old houses and flats could be pulled down.

Teacher: Thank you. Now who is going to speak against the proposal?

Child D: I am. I think we should not build lots of new houses in this country. I think it is a bad idea for many reasons. For a start, houses are often built on farmland or other green spaces. If we build lots of houses then trees will be cut down and fields and hedges will be lost. Animals will lose their homes and there will not be so many good places for people to go for walks. Another reason that I am against building lots of houses is that it will mean more roads. More roads means more cars and more noise and pollution.

Teacher: Thank you. Does anybody else wish to speak against the suggestion?

Child E: Yes, I do. I know someone who lives near a big estate of new houses that were built last year. He says that the view from his house is now spoiled and that the roads there are now clogged with traffic because of all the extra people. The shops are too busy and all the local schools are overcrowded. It has spoiled the town. Do we want this to happen all over our country?

Teacher: Thank you. All the speakers have done very well and given some good reasons for and against the proposal to build lots of new houses in Britain. Now we must decide what to do. The fairest way is to have a vote. Everyone in the hall has one vote. So, put up your hand if you think we should build lots of new houses in this country. Hands down. Now put up your hand if you think we should not build lots of new houses in this country. [*Decide if there needs to be a count.*] The result is _______.

So that is how a debate works. We can't really decide what to do about important things like building houses but important people in the Houses of Parliament have debates like ours and they do decide real things. Maybe one day you'll be one of the people who decides things.

Interactive Follow-up

Questions

1) What was the debate about?
   (Whether to build lots of new houses in Britain.)
2) The people who made the proposal wanted to build new houses – why?
   (1. To house the homeless; 2. To provide low-cost housing for young people; 3. To provide jobs; 4. To replace old, unsuitable housing.)
3) What did the people against building new houses say?
   (1. They would cause environmental damage; 2. They would cause overcrowding and noise; 3. They would reduce people's quality of life, e.g. through loss of green spaces.)

Getting the message

The children speaking in this debate were reading out from a script, so they weren't really giving their own views. In a real debate, everyone has a chance to say what they think. Which of these things should happen in a real debate? Nod your head for the ones that are:

- Listening
- Speaking
- Shouting
- Voting
- Giving your opinion
- Having arguments

Learning more

What do we call the people who have important debates in the Houses of Parliament in London? *(MPs and Lords, some of whom are members of the government.)*

Non-interactive Follow-up

Summary

- The debate is about building houses in Britain.
- One person proposed that we should build new houses.
- Another person agreed and gave reasons why they thought it was a good idea.
- A third person also agreed with building new houses and gave another reason.
- Someone else was against the idea: this person gave several reasons for not building new houses in Britain.
- Another person agreed and said why it was not a good idea in their opinion.
- At the end, there was a vote to see what everyone thought.

Reflection

Taking part in a debate is a good thing. Try to learn to have your say and speak up for what you believe is right. Listen to others and think about what they say: always be ready to change your mind and to be fair. Next time there's a classroom debate, try to join in.

Prayer

Lord God, thank you that we have debates in our country to decide important things like whether or not to build lots of new houses. Help us to listen to each other, to think hard and to make wise choices. Help us to join in the debates we have at school and to have our say. Amen.

2c Recognising choices: It's Your Choice

Objective

To help children recognise the choices they can make and the differences between right and wrong.

PSHE/Citizenship links

2c: recognising choices.

Props

(Not essential): a bar of chocolate

Introduction

Today's assembly is all about choices. Sometimes we make a good choice and sometimes we make a bad choice. Sometimes it's hard to know what's right and what's wrong. The author of this story has looked back on his life and thought about some of the choices that he made when he was younger. It's an interesting story.

Story: It's Your Choice

One of the silliest things that children do is to blame other people when they get into trouble. Yes, alright, sometimes it is somebody else's fault when you're in trouble, but often it's your own fault. I'll show you what I mean: these are all things that happened to me.

When I was very young, I remember getting a selection box for Christmas, you know, one of those big boxes full of different kinds of chocolate bars. It was there at the bottom of my bed on Christmas morning. I opened it then woke up my sister to see if she'd got one too. It was really early in the morning and our parents were still fast asleep. I remember my sister daring me to eat all of the selection box. "There's no one to stop us," she said.

I ate a Crunchie, a bar of chocolate and a Twix. I started to eat some Buttons but then I started to feel sick. I couldn't eat my Christmas dinner that day and my parents were furious. I tried to blame my sister but it was me that ate all the chocolate – it was my choice and I chose the wrong thing to do. Two weeks later, I didn't have any chocolate left when I really wanted some.

I remember another time, when I was at school. There was this new boy who joined the class. He was called Danny, I think. He was overweight, and people started to point at him and laugh and call him fat. I did it too, sometimes, I'm ashamed to say. The really sad thing was that he didn't really make any friends for a while. At playtimes, he just wandered around on his own. He didn't like football or the chasing games we used to play, so we just left him out.

Now, when I think about those things and the way we treated Danny, it was really cruel. He was a nice boy, too. I was wrong to make fun of him and call him names. I had a choice: I knew that the right thing to do was to make friends with Danny and be kind to him. I should have thought how I would have felt if I had moved to a new school and had no friends. I had a choice, but I chose the wrong thing again. I really regret it now.

When I was a little older and in the juniors, I joined up with a gang of boys who were often in trouble. I knew it probably wasn't a good idea hanging around with them but it felt cool at the time. We used to go to a park near my house. It had a good adventure playground and hills where we could race our bikes, I recall. When we got bored with the swings and playing on our bikes, we used to go to the pets' corner.

The pets' corner was a place for younger children. It had big cages with birds and rabbits and guinea pigs and chickens. I think they had a goat there, too, once. We didn't go there to look at the animals, though – we used to scare them by shouting and we even threw stones at the rabbits once. It was a cruel thing to do, I know. I can't believe I used to do things like that, but when you're young you often make the wrong choices. It was wrong for me to join in with those boys and it was wrong for me to scare those animals. I'm really sorry that I did it.

When I was twelve or so, I had to go to a big secondary school, which was much further from my house than my first school. I walked there in the morning with a friend and it was quite a long way. There was a shortcut across a farmer's field that we used to take. It wasn't a proper footpath, though. We used to climb the fence and walk across the field instead of going round it like we should have done. Eventually, the old wooden fence broke and there was a gap. Lots of people started using the shortcut and dogs used to get in there.

I remember that the farmer put some sheep in the field next door, but they got out through a gate that someone left open and they walked into the field that we used for our shortcut. Some sheep strayed through the gap in the fence we had made and wandered onto the road, nearly causing a nasty accident with two cars. The police came and the farmer had to mend the fence. But it was our fault. We shouldn't have walked across that field – I now know that that's called trespassing, when you go onto someone else's land without permission where there's no public footpath. It was another wrong choice. I should have done the right thing and walked around. Someone could have been really badly hurt in that road accident.

I think the worse thing I did when I was younger was to take something that didn't belong to me. My dad had a drawer in my parents' bedroom where he kept all of his loose change: all the coins that he had in his pockets at the end of each day. I remember that he used to count it up after a while and put it into small polythene bags and take it to the bank. Sometimes there were hundreds and hundreds of coins in there: fifty pence pieces, tens and fives, plus loads of two pence coins and ones. This was a long while ago, before there were pound coins or twenty pence pieces.

I was hanging around with some friends who used to go to a shop at weekends to buy coke and sweets. They always seemed to have more pocket money than I did and often I couldn't afford to buy anything. One day, I took some money from my dad's drawer to buy a can of drink. I knew it was wrong. I was stealing. I did it again too... and again. Each time, I had to make the choice and I chose badly. I didn't get caught, but now I so much regret doing it. I have a terrible feeling inside me even when I think about it: grown ups call it guilt.

I hope that, when you grow up, you won't look back like I am now and remember all the bad choices you made. I did make right choices too, but not enough of them, and I'm really sorry.

Interactive Follow-up

Questions

1) Why did the author regret eating all those chocolates?
   (He felt sick; he got into trouble; he missed his Christmas dinner; his chocolate was all gone quickly.)
2) Who was Danny and what happened to him?
   (He was a new boy at the author's school; he was called names and laughed at; he didn't have any friends.)
3) Why does the author say that he made a bad choice each time?
   (Because he now knows that what he did was wrong.)

Getting the message

1) How can you tell what is right and what is wrong? (*open-ended*)
2) Put your hand up if you agree with these statements:
   - We all make mistakes sometimes.
   - It's a good idea to blame someone else if you're in trouble.
   - If you tell lies then people won't believe you, even when you tell the truth later on.
   - Laughing at people is harmless.
   - It's hard not to join in if your friends are doing something wrong.
   - You should always think before you make a choice.

Learning more

If you do make a bad choice and do something wrong, what should you do afterwards?

Non-interactive Follow-up

Summary

- The author of the story looked back at some of the bad choices he had made.
- He said it was wrong to blame other people when you get into trouble.
- He ate too much chocolate at Christmas as a child and regretted it.
- He also joined in making fun of a new boy called Danny, who was overweight and lonely.
- He told the story of how he trespassed across a farmer's field to get to school and nearly caused a serious road accident.
- He also mentioned being cruel to animals in a park, another wrong choice which he's sorry about.
- Finally, he described stealing money from his dad to pay for cans of drink – he felt very bad about this looking back, because he knows it was wrong.

Something to think about

Some people say that, if you do the right thing, you feel good about it afterwards. This can be true, even if it's not what you want to do at the time.

Reflection

Right or wrong – it's your choice. We all have to make lots of choices every single day of our lives. If you make the wrong choices then you can get into trouble and you may regret it. If you do what is right, you'll feel good about it and you'll probably be helping others too. Think before you make your choices.

Prayer

Lord God, thank you that we can make choices in our lives. Please help us to make the right choices every day. Teach us what is right and what is wrong, and help us to choose what's right every time, even if it's not always what we want. Amen.

2D Following rules: "Don't"

Objective

To increase awareness of the role and usefulness of rules, and to relate this to rules that govern everyday life.

PSHE/Citizenship links

2d: following rules for the children's group and their classroom and understanding how rules help them.

Props

(Not essential): anything that is mentioned in the poem, e.g. a gravy boat, some confetti or some fruit.

Introduction

Do you get fed up with people saying "Don't do this!" and "Don't do that!"? Sometimes it seems that the whole world is made up of rules about things you aren't allowed to do. Today's poem, by Michael Rosen, is about a boy who is very fed up with being told not to do things.

Poem: "Don't" by Michael Rosen

Don't do,
Don't do,
Don't do that.
Don't pull faces,
Don't tease the cat.

Don't pick your ears,
Don't be rude at school.
Who do they think I am?

Some kind of fool?

One day they'll say
Don't put toffee in my coffee
Don't pour gravy on the baby
Don't put beer in his ear
Don't stick your toes up his nose.

Don't put confetti on the spaghetti
And don't squash peas on your knees.

Don't put ants in your pants
Don't put mustard in the custard

Don't chuck jelly at the telly

And don't throw fruit at the computer
Don't throw fruit at the computer.

Don't what?
Don't throw fruit at the computer.
Don't what?
Don't throw fruit at the computer.
Who do they think I am?
Some kind of fool?

["Don't" by Michael Rosen from *Don't Put Mustard in the Custard* (© Michael Rosen 1985) is reproduced by permission of PFD (www.pfd.co.uk) on behalf of Michael Rosen.]

Interactive Follow-up

Questions

The boy in the poem was really fed up with being told what he wasn't allowed to do.

1) Listen to the first bit again and tell me the four things he's told not to do.
   (Re-read the first two verses: pulling faces, teasing the cat, picking his ears, being rude at school.)
2) What do you think of those rules? Give me a thumbs up, like this, if you think that they're quite sensible rules to have and a thumbs down, like this, if you think that they are bad rules.
   (Go through them individually and ask for opinions on why they are good or bad rules, e.g. picking your ears doesn't look good and it can make them sore, so it's probably quite a good rule, etc.)

Getting the message

A lot of rules we have in school are very good rules. Can you think of some? *(If time permits, you could ask for a few children with ideas about good rules to come and stand at the front and tell everyone their suggestions. Examples might be: not running in the corridors, being helpful and polite, not talking when other people are talking, etc.)*

Learning more

Now let's look again at some of the very silly rules that the boy thinks the grown ups around him might come up with next. *(Re-read however much of the rest of the poem will fit in time-wise, pausing after each 'rule' to invite comment: all are rules that are 'correct', but so silly that we probably wouldn't break them anyhow.)*

Non-interactive Follow-up

Summary

- A poem about a boy who is frequently told what he is not allowed to do.
- He isn't allowed to pull faces, tease his cat, pick his ears or be rude at school.
- He starts to wonder what sort of daft rules the adults around him will make up next.
- He imagines rules about pouring gravy on babies and pouring beer in their ears, etc.
- He points out that he doesn't really need telling what's sensible and what isn't.

Reflection

Learning lots of different rules can be quite hard. A very good rule that you can use in lots of different situations is to treat other people in exactly the same way as you'd like to be treated yourself. For example, if you wouldn't like someone to knock you over in the corridor when they were running, then don't run yourself; if you'd like people to listen carefully to what you have to say, then make sure you listen carefully to other people.

Prayer

Lord God, thank you that there are rules at school that keep us safe and make sure that things are fair. Help us to stick to the rules so that we can all enjoy our life here together. Remind us to always treat others just the same as we would like them to treat us. Amen.

2E MEETING NEEDS: THE NEW BABY

Objective

To help the children to understand that people in general, and babies in particular, have needs; also, that it is our responsibility to try to meet the needs of others.

PSHE/Citizenship links

2e: to realise that people and other living things have needs, and that they have responsibilities to meet them.

Props

(Not essential): a picture of a baby, some baby toys and nappies and a football

Introduction

How many of you have little brothers and sisters? Some of you might even have one on the way right now and are looking forward to having a new baby in the house. It's really exciting when a new baby arrives but, when it does, you soon learn that it needs a lot of care. Today's story is all about a new baby in the family.

STORY: THE NEW BABY

Reuben was SO excited! When he woke up that morning, he found that his mum and dad weren't at home, and that his gran had suddenly appeared from nowhere. That could only mean one thing – Dad had taken Mum to the hospital to have their new baby!

Reuben's teacher, Mrs Stone, knew that he was going to have a new brother or sister, because he had hardly stopped talking about it for the last few weeks. So she wasn't one bit surprised when he couldn't really settle down to his number work that morning. It was a long day for him at school that day and he didn't really listen properly to the story at the end of the day, even though that was his favourite thing. When the end of school came, Mrs Stone let Reuben out before all of the others – even before the bus children – so that he could dash out to where his gran was waiting at the school gate.

She was smiling her best smile, so Reuben knew that the baby must have been born during the day. "Oh, what is it? What is it, Gran?" he burst out impatiently. "Tell me, QUICK!"

"Well, I will, if you give me half a chance!" she laughed. "It's a little boy and he's going to be called Sam."

"Wahoo!" shouted Reuben. "I KNEW it would be! When can I see him?"

"Dad says that we can go round to the hospital straight away, if you like," said Gran.

The next day at school, Mrs Stone asked Reuben to tell the class all about his new baby brother. "Well, he's teeny-weeny and I was allowed to hold him very carefully, while I sat on the chair next to Mum's bed. He woke up and looked at me, and I think he liked me. It's going to be great to have a brother, because it'll be someone to play with and I can teach him football and we can play pirates together!"

"You'll have to help your mum with him as well, though," said Mrs Stone. "Babies take a lot of looking after, you know, especially at first."

"Oh yes," said Reuben, "I know all about that – I'm going to help bathe him and change his nappy and all that: Mum's going to teach me."

Mum stayed in hospital for a couple of days, and Gran and Reuben made them welcome home cards and decorated Sam's room with all the cards that their friends and family had sent. Reuben couldn't WAIT for them to come home: it was going to be so cool!

The first evening, Reuben wanted to give Sam a bath, but he was too sleepy, so Reuben had to make do with having a big cuddle with him. The next morning, Mum was very tired, because Sam had been crying a lot in the night. She wasn't her usual, cheerful self at all, and Sam just cried when she wasn't holding him. Reuben tried to cheer him up by telling him a story, but it didn't work: he just kept on crying. Things hadn't got much better by the time Reuben came home from school again, and Mum didn't have time to hear him read from his new book. Gran heard him instead, but it wasn't the same at all.

In fact, all sorts of things weren't the same anymore. Mum and Dad seemed tired all the time; they nearly always had quick meals: the sort mum could just shove in the oven without having to do much cooking; whenever Reuben wanted to do something, he found that the baby needed changing or feeding or winding, and it never seemed to be his turn for anything any more.

The whole thing wasn't half as much fun as he'd thought it was going to be, and he was very sad. It would have been better if Sam hadn't come at all. All he did was sleep and cry – and Reuben was sure he did more crying than sleeping – and it wasn't AT ALL how he'd imagined it.

One evening, he was sitting in a sulky heap on the settee, while mum was changing Sam's nappy AGAIN (it must have been at least the hundredth time that day, thought Reuben) and he found a big, fat tear rolling down his cheek. Mum spotted it and said, "What's up, Reub? Are you poorly?" She handed Sam over to Dad, and came and sat with Reuben.

Soon it all came pouring out: how excited Reuben had been, but how Sam had spoiled all of his great plans. He couldn't play football or pirates and, when Reuben tried to help, all Sam did was cry and want Mum, so Mum spent all her time with the horrid baby, and... and... and Reuben couldn't say any more, because he was crying so much.

Mum gave him a great big hug. "Poor old Reub. It's very hard when a new baby comes into the house – it's hard for everyone, not just you. Dad and I are very tired, because he needs so much care and attention – even at night time, when we should all be fast asleep!"

"He needs so much that it doesn't seem worth it," sniffed Reuben. "He doesn't actually DO anything and he's no fun at all, so why do you bother with him? Can't we just get rid of him again?"

Mum laughed. "Oh, Reub! You can't get rid of a baby, just because he needs lots of things! Babies are people, you know, just like you and me. They just can't do things for themselves yet. You were exactly the same, you know, when you were a baby. Dad and I had to spend lots of sleepless nights looking after you, we had to change hundreds of your nappies, and it was AGES before you were big enough to play football and pirates. Sam won't be like this forever and, as he grows up, you'll be able to do lots of fun things together. But while he's tiny, just like you used to be, he needs us to do lots of things for him to help him grow up. If we don't help him, who will?"

And Mum was quite right. Soon Sam was able to do more things, and he really loved his big brother. Reuben found ways of playing with him that Sam could manage and they began to have real fun together. Sometimes they argued, too, but they grew up being the best of friends. Having a brother was actually even better than Reuben had thought it could be, and that's saying something!

Interactive Follow-up

Questions

1) Why was Reuben so excited about having a new baby?
   (He thought it was going to be huge fun to have a brother or sister to play with.)
2) What sort of things did he want to do with Sam, when he'd been born?
   (He wanted to play pirates with him and teach him football.)
3) What did Mrs Stone tell him he'd have to do?
   (She told him he'd have to help out with the baby, because they need a lot of care, especially when they're tiny.)
4) How was it different to how Reuben had imagined it?
   (There was no time for him any more; Sam couldn't play with him as he'd hoped he would; he wasn't even able to help as much as he'd thought, because Sam cried and wanted his mum.)
5) How did it all turn out in the end?
   (Reuben accepted that Sam had a lot of needs and the two of them grew up to be the best of friends.)

Getting the message

Sam seemed to need so many things. Put your hands up when you hear something that a new baby might need:

- patience
- feeding
- chips and beef burgers
- cuddles
- nappies changing
- to learn the rules of football

Learning more

Mum said that babies are people, just like we are. Let's think of the sorts of things we all need. I've got some ideas here. Show me 10 fingers if you think what I say is very important for us to have, five fingers if you think it's quite important and no fingers if you don't think we need it at all.

- love and patience
- good food
- very expensive toys
- sleep
- people to listen to us
- a pet elephant

How many of those things can you give to other people who might need them? *(All of us can give love and patience and be prepared to listen to others.)*

Non-interactive Follow-up

Summary

- Reuben was very excited because he was going to have a baby brother or sister.
- He was very pleased when Sam was born and had plans for them to do exciting things together.
- Things didn't go according to Reuben's plans, as Sam couldn't play and needed so many things from the family.
- Reuben became upset and wished that Sam would go away again.
- Mum told him that it had been exactly the same when he was first born.
- She reassured him and, in the end, having a brother was even better than Reuben had thought it was going to be.

Reflection

All of us need looking after and caring for in different ways, whether we're tiny babies, school children or grown up. No one can meet ALL the needs that other people have, but we can all try our best to help meet some of them. Think about people in your family and people in your class: how might you help them today?

Prayer

Lord God, thank you that you know all of our needs and that you look after us every day. Please help us to spot when somebody close to us needs something and help us to do our best to help them. Amen.

2F BELONGING: WE BELONG

Objective

To help children understand that they belong to various groups and communities.

PSHE/Citizenship links

2f: belonging.

Preparation

This assembly is in the form of a whole class presentation. The class will need to stand at the front of the hall in four groups (G1-G4) and read out lines from a script together, as in choral speaking. Children will need a copy of the script each and some rehearsal time. There are actions to carry out as well as words to read, and a few props are needed. The name of the local village, town or city will need to be inserted into G4's first line.

Props

Globe or large world map, Union Jack flags on sticks (can be home-made), large sign or banner with the name of the village/town/city where the school is situated, banner with the name of the class on it, photos of families.

Introduction

It's good to belong to something. But what exactly do we belong to? Today, our class is going to answer that question.

DRAMA SCRIPT: WE BELONG

G1 We all belong to the world *[make big circle with arms]* – it's our planet.

G2 We are all Europeans too – we belong to the continent of Europe. *[Point to Europe on map or globe.]*

G3 We all live in Britain, so we belong to this country. *[Wave flags.]*

G4 We also belong to . . . . , because we live here. *[Hold up banner.]*

G1 We are all part of our school too – we belong to it. *[Hold out arms with palms up.]*

G2 We belong to our class because we are all members of it. *[Hold up class banner.]*

G3 At home, we belong to our families and they belong to us. *[Hold up photos of families.]*

G4 We belong to lots of other groups too.

G1 The football team.

G2 The rounders team.

G3 Brownies.

G4 Cubs.

G1 My church.
G2 My mosque.
G3 A recorder group.
G4 A choir.
G1 The RSPB Junior Birdwatchers' club.
G2 The Beano fan club.
G3 A swimming club.
G4 A gym club.
All And there are lots and lots of other places we can belong to too. It's good to belong!

Interactive Follow-up

Questions

1) What are some of the things that everyone belongs to?
(The school; the world, etc.)
2) What else do the children in this class belong to?
(Families, clubs, etc.)
3) Why do you think the children said that "It's good to belong"?
(So you don't get bored or lonely; it makes you feel special.)

Getting the message

Put your hand up if you belong to one of these:

- A class in this school.
- A school club or group.
- A team.
- A sports club.
- A church or mosque.
- A country.
- Brownies or cubs.

Non-interactive Follow-up

Summary

- The class talked about the things they belonged to.
- They belong to the world and to Europe and Britain.
- They are a part of a school and a class.
- They belong to a family.
- They also belong to clubs and groups – it feels good to belong to something.

Something to think about

It's fun to join a club or a group – why not go along with someone who already belongs to one and see what it's like?

Reflection

We all belong to lots of different groups and communities. It's good to belong – we feel part of something and we are not alone. We can share with others who also belong. As you get older, think about belonging to some new and different groups: you'll enjoy it.

Prayer

Lord God, thank you for this school that we belong to and our class and our families too. Thank you for all the other places that we belong as well, such as clubs and groups. Help us to be kind towards people who don't belong and to encourage them to join in. Amen.

2G IMPROVING THE ENVIRONMENT: THE DAY THE STUDENTS CAME

Objective
To raise awareness of environmental issues, and that we can all make a difference to our local environment, wherever we live.

PSHE/Citizenship links
2g: looking after the local environment.

Props
None

Introduction
Today's story is about a girl who lives in a place which makes her sad, until one day a quite unexpected thing happens.

STORY: THE DAY THE STUDENTS CAME

The sun was shining when Li woke up. It was a beautiful day and it was a Saturday too. That meant no school – she could go out and play with her friends. After grabbing some toast, Li rushed outside to see who was around on the estate. There was a black dog trotting across the grass by the road but there were no children there. There were none at the swings either, which was a shame because it was such a wonderful day: warm and clear and sunny.

Li crossed the road and the grass to the swings. She would wait there – one of her friends was bound to turn up soon. There was only one swing working in the children's play area. The rest had all been vandalised: broken by older kids who were bored in the evenings, probably. She knew the names of some of them – they were always in trouble. Li sat on the swing and rocked back and forth, waiting. As she waited, she looked around at the neighbourhood where she lived.

Li lived in a big city called Manchester, on a large housing estate. There were blocks of flats next to rows of old houses. Some of these houses were being knocked down and there were metal fences with 'Keep Out' signs around them. Some new houses had been built but a lot of them had ugly graffiti sprayed on the walls. Li didn't really like her neighbourhood.

At least there was the big grassy area where she was now. But even this was spoiled. The children's play equipment was nearly all damaged and there were broken bottles and litter everywhere. The fence to keep dogs out had been smashed in three places and everything looked so sad and ugly.

Across the other side of the grass was the remains of a fire. There were supermarket trolleys on it and more rubbish. Nearby, a rusty old car had been abandoned on the grass. Its windows were smashed. Behind this part of the grassy area was a garden which the council had built a year ago. When it was new, it had brick beds full of colourful flowers and paths and trees planted in between. Now these trees were all dead – snapped off by someone who just wanted to do damage. The flowers were mostly gone, too, and even one of the brick walls had been knocked over.

Li felt really miserable. Why didn't anybody care about this neighbourhood? It was really sad. Just then Li heard her name being called from behind. It was her friend, Kelly.

"Hey Li, have you seen what the students are doing?"

"What students?" said Li. She didn't know what Kelly meant at all.

"I've just been to Howden Street with the other kids. There's all these students there, cleaning up the place. And they're coming here now. They've got vans and wheelbarrows and all sorts of stuff!" Li was just about to ask Kelly to slow down and explain again, when both girls heard an engine and turned round to see three vans pull up on the edge of the grassy area.

"It's them!" shouted Kelly, running off towards the vans. "Come on!"

Li followed her friend over to the vans. She watched about thirty young people climb out. "These must be the students," she thought to herself. Each one of them carried something: a rubbish bag, a spade, a wheelbarrow, a brush, a box or a rake. A girl who looked about nineteen smiled at Li as she walked past. Li wanted to ask her what they were doing but she knew that she shouldn't talk to strangers.

A group of the students, all young men, went over to one of the walls which was covered in spray paint. Right away, they took out some cans from the boxes they were carrying and some brushes and they started to clean off the ugly graffiti. They joked and laughed as they worked. Li noticed that they were all wearing the same blue t-shirt. It had a message written on it, although Li couldn't see what it said.

Kelly came over again and said, "Look." Li turned around and saw that there were groups of students all over the grassy area, working and cleaning it up. Some were in the garden, planting new flowers and trees and mending the broken wall. Others were fixing the fence around the play area, hammering new pieces of wood into place, while another group were cleaning up the play equipment as best they could. It was simply amazing.

The rusty car was soon pushed away off the grass over to where the houses were being knocked down. The piles of burnt rubbish on the bonfire were taken away, along with the supermarket trolleys and all of the dangerous bits of metal. Bags and bags of crisp packets, glass bottles, cans and take-away litter were collected and put into the vans.

"Why are they doing it?" said Li to Kelly, who seemed to know so much.

"My big sister asked them and they told her that it's a community project. They're all students who are at a festival in Manchester and they all wanted to help clean up the city this weekend."

"So it's not just our neighbourhood they're doing?" said Li.

"The students said that there are three thousand of them working all around the city."

"Wow!" said Li. "I hope it doesn't all go back to how it was before."

"When I'm older," said Kelly, "I'm going to do what they're doing."

"Me too," said Li. "Me too."

INTERACTIVE FOLLOW-UP

Questions

1) In what kind of place did Li live? *(A housing estate in a big city.)*
2) What was Li's neighbourhood like?
   (It was in a bad way: full of litter and graffiti and mess, with vandalism and destruction.)
3) What were the students doing there?
   (Cleaning up the neighbourhood as best they could; mending things and making it look better.)
4) Why did the students do this?
   (It was a community project: they wanted to help clean up the city where they were having a festival; they did it to help others.)

Getting the message

1) Why did Kelly and Li want to do what the students were doing? *(Because it looked fun and also because they were making a difference to the community and the environment.)*
2) Wherever we live, there are plenty of things we can do to look after and improve our neighbourhood. Give me a thumbs up for things that help to look after our environment and a thumbs down for things that harm it:
   - Dropping litter.
   - Clearing up the mess our dogs leave when we take them out for a walk.
   - Giving spare change to organisations who look after stray animals.
   - Wasting electricity by leaving lights and the TV on when no one's even in the room.
   - Feeding garden birds during the cold months of winter, when they can't find much food for themselves.

Learning more

Why do people drop litter and what can be done to stop it happening?

Non-interactive Follow-up

Summary

- Li went outside on a sunny day to the playground near her home.
- She lived on an estate in a big city called Manchester.
- Lots of things about the neighbourhood were bad.
- The play equipment was vandalised and there was littler and graffiti everywhere.
- Li and her friend Kelly watched some students arrive in three vans.
- The students cleaned up the litter and repaired things like fences.
- They worked on the garden and fixed the play equipment as part of a community project.
- The students made the neighbourhood much nicer.
- Li and Kelly wanted to do what the students did when they grew up.

Reflection

The students in the story made a wonderful difference to Li and Kelly's neighbourhood. But vans and wheelbarrows and huge teams of people aren't the only way to make an environment better. We can all do it by not dropping litter, by looking after play equipment and by caring for the places around us. We can all make a difference.

Prayer

Lord God, thank you for our neighbourhoods, wherever we live. Help us to understand how important it is for us to look after them and not to spoil them. Please help us to grow up caring about our environment and making a difference for the better. Amen.

2H Making a contribution: Hans Holds Back the Sea

Objective

To help children appreciate how different people can make different kinds of contributions to the life of a class or school.

PSHE/Citizenship links

2h: contributing to the life of the class or school.

Props

None

Introduction

Sometimes, grown ups like teachers talk about "making a contribution". But what is a contribution and how do you make one? Well, a contribution is actually something that you give. It means when you do something good that helps other people in some way. For example, you can contribute money to a charity, such as Oxfam or Help the Aged – that means you give them some money so that they can use it to help people in need. You can also contribute time – that means that you spend time with a person who likes your company, a grandparent maybe, or do something useful around the house perhaps. There are lots and lots of ways that people contribute to help others. There's a famous story about a little boy who once made a small contribution that turned out to be very important.

Story: Hans Holds Back the Sea

The boy, so the story goes, called Hans, lived in Holland a long time ago. Now Holland is a small country, not too far from our country, across the sea. In fact, it is right next to the sea. Holland is famous for being a very flat place. It has very good farmland where they grow flowers and vegetables – the Dutch people, as they are called, are especially good at growing tulips.

Now Hans lived in a small house near the sea. His father was a lockkeeper, who looked after one of the canals which criss-cross the country. Canals are like rivers, which have been built by people so that boats can travel around the country. Hans used to watch his father letting boats through the canals and he also used to watch the wild North Sea. To see the sea, Hans had to climb up on a special huge wall called a dyke. The dykes are very important in Holland because they stop the sea from flooding the land. In many parts of Holland, the land is actually lower than the sea and only the great earth dykes hold it back.

One evening, Hans was walking along the dyke all alone when he heard a strange noise, a trickling sound. He looked down the side of the dyke and saw that there was water leaking through the sea wall. Like every Dutch boy and girl, Hans knew that this meant danger. If the sea was leaking through, there must be a hole in the dyke. When the tide came in, it would make the hole bigger and break open the wall. The land would be flooded and people might even be drowned. It had happened before.

Hans screamed at the top of his voice, "Help! Help! Come quick, someone – there is a leak in the dyke! Help!" He called and he shouted but there was no one about. It was getting dark now and everyone had gone indoors. He was the only one who knew about the danger. Hans scuttled down the steep slope of the dyke wall and went to have a closer look at the leak. There was a small hole and sea water was gushing though it. Hans looked around again, but there was no one there. He put his finger in the hole and the water stopped. It was cold, and soon his finger began to ache, but Hans knew that he had to stay there until someone came along.

Ten minutes passed and then half an hour and then an hour. No one came, not a soul. It was now dark, and poor Hans was so cold and uncomfortable that he moaned and cried. He longed to take his finger out of the dyke and run home to his warm, comfortable bed, but he knew that he could not. Hans stayed and he passed the whole night, holding back the sea, protecting the land and the people of Holland.

Hans couldn't sleep at all that night and he was greatly relieved to see the first light of dawn in the morning. His body was now numb with cold and he couldn't feel his finger at all. He twisted around again to try to get comfortable and, as he did so, he heard a sound: whistling, someone whistling. A moment later, a man appeared on the dyke, riding his bicycle. It was the pastor of the local church! Hans called out and the man stopped and looked down into the gloom.

"Hans? Is that you? Whatever are you doing down there?" He hopped off his bike and hurried down the dyke to see if Hans was alright. Hans could barely speak, but the pastor saw his finger in the wall and realised right away what had happened. Within an hour, a group of people arrived and fixed the hole in the dyke. Hans was carried home to his worried family. He had saved the land. He was a hero.

That story is well known across the world, but it's not actually true. It was written in a book by an author who lived in America, but it's still a good way of explaining how a small contribution can be a big help. Hans was a hero, a great person, because he made a special contribution to helping others. Sticking your finger in a hole doesn't seem like much, but doing it all night when you're cold and in pain is very brave.

We don't have any dykes here, and the sea isn't about to flood our land – well, I hope not, anyway, but we can all make a contribution. We can make a contribution in class by answering questions and by joining in discussions. We can make a contribution in school by offering to help someone with something, by being kind to someone who is sad or by playing with someone who is lonely in the playground.

There are lots and lots of other ways to make a contribution too. See if you can find some today and every day of this week.

Interactive Follow-up

Questions

1) What is a dyke?
   (A big sea wall found in Holland, built to protect low-lying land from flooding.)
2) Why did Hans stick his finger in the dyke?
   (To plug a leak which could have become a serious flood.)
3) Why did Hans become a hero?
   (Because he prevented what may have been a disaster, with land flooded and possibly people drowned.)

Getting the message

1) Hans made a great contribution to his community – what does that mean?
2) The story was all about making a contribution by doing something to help others. Put your thumb up if I say something which is a good contribution to your class:
   - Answering a question.
   - Calling out.
   - Doing someone's work for them.
   - Saying a kind word to someone.
   - Helping to wash up paint pots.
   - Picking things up off the floor.

Non-interactive Follow-up

Summary

- Hans lived in Holland, a flat country by the sea.
- Hans went on a walk along a dyke, which is a big wall built to stop the low land from flooding.
- Hans saw that there was a leak in the dyke and he called for help.
- No one was around so Hans plugged the leak with his finger, because he knew that there could be a serious flood if he didn't.
- He spent all night with his finger in the dyke.
- The church pastor found him in the morning, exhausted and cold.
- The dyke leak was mended and Hans became a local hero.
- The story is not true but it is a good illustration of how one person can make a contribution which helps others, even though it's not always a pleasant thing to do.

Something to think about

What do others think about people who make a contribution?

Reflection

Hans made a big contribution to his community but even small contributions are important. Try hard to make a contribution to your class and to your school, and also try to value other peoples' contributions too.

Prayer

Lord God, thank you that we can all make a contribution to our school community in different ways. Help us to think of ways that we can help each other and become involved in making our class and our school a good place to be. Amen.

2I Where money comes from and goes to: Money

Objective

To make children aware that suddenly having a great deal of money and being able to buy smart new things doesn't necessarily lead to happiness. Sometimes using money for things we think we want, but don't necessarily need, leads to discontent.

PSHE/Citizenship links

2i: to realise that money comes from different sources and can be used for different purposes.

Props

(Not essential): a goose egg sprayed gold

Introduction

Do you ever wonder what you would do if you suddenly had lots of money to spend? I often do. I'd probably get rid of my old kitchen table and get a nice new one; and I think I might change my car for a smarter model. The trouble is, then they would make lots of my other things look old and tatty, so I'd end up having to get lots and LOTS of nice new things. I wonder if that would make me any happier, though? This story might help to answer that question…

Story: Money

Frank and Freda were a happy couple; they lived on a little farm not too far away from the town. Their farm used to be a very busy place, but now that they were old, Frank and Freda only kept a few sheep, one enormous, friendly pig called Hector and a small flock of geese. The animals gave them just enough work to do to keep them busy and brought in just enough money for what they needed. They really enjoyed their life together.

Each morning, Frank would go out into the yard with the pig bucket and give Hector his breakfast. Hector was always pleased to see him and loved it when Frank scratched his back while he slurped and grunted his way through his delicious slops. Once Frank had given Hector fresh straw and clean water, he would go across the yard to let the geese out. There would usually be a freshly laid egg in the goose hut and Frank would take it back to the farmhouse, after he'd fed the geese and let them out for the day. Goose eggs are far bigger than hens' eggs, so Frank and Freda would share one for their breakfast.

One morning, Freda was just getting out the pan ready to cook that day's egg, when she saw Frank walking across the yard with a puzzled expression on his face, scratching his head. He held an egg in his hand as usual, but he was staring and staring at it: there was definitely something about the egg that was bothering him.

"Well, I'll be blowed..." was all he could mutter as he came through the kitchen door, still scratching his head, "if that goose hasn't gone and laid us a golden egg!" Freda looked and Frank was right – there in his hand lay an egg made of pure gold! They were very excited and, instead of cooking their usual breakfast, they went straight into town and had breakfast at a smart café to celebrate.

To their amazement, the eggs just kept on coming and coming and coming, until they had so much money they hardly knew what to do with it all. After a while, Freda stopped cooking altogether and they went and had all of their meals at cafés and restaurants. They noticed that their old clothes were a bit tatty for visiting such smart places, so they bought whole sets of new ones. They also bought new carpets and curtains, furniture and a brand new car – each – even though there was nothing wrong with their old things. All this spending meant that they didn't have time for their ordinary farm work any more, so they sold their sheep and Hector the pig, as well as most of the geese. They kept the one that laid the golden eggs, of course.

Then, one morning, when Frank went out to collect that day's golden egg, he was surprised to find no egg at all – not even an ordinary one. He and Freda didn't think too much about it though, because they were just about to go into town to choose an expensive new bathroom. There would be another again tomorrow, they told each other as they hopped into one of the new cars. But there wasn't. Or the next day. Or the next. Freda began to get worried and soon they were both very cross with the goose.

"This just isn't good enough!" said Freda. "That goose needs teaching a lesson! She's started keeping all those golden eggs to herself and I'm not having it!"

"No, it's not right," agreed Fred. "But what shall we do?"

"There's only one thing for it," said Freda. "We'll have to cut her open and get them all out ourselves." And that's just what they did. Frank killed the goose and cut her open. And how many golden eggs do you think they found inside? One? Three? Ten? Actually, they didn't find any at all. And, of course, now their precious goose was dead and would never lay any sort of eggs again. When they saw what they had done, they suddenly felt very sad – and very stupid.

"We have been really silly," groaned Frank. "We were perfectly happy before we had all this money, but we still changed our lives, just because we were suddenly rich. I don't know about you, but I wish everything could go back to how it was before."

"I agree," said Freda. "I'm really bored with eating out at posh places and spending half of my life at the hairdresser's and in shops. Let's get back to our old, comfy way of life and forget this ever happened."

And that's exactly what they did. They sold their new cars, bought a little flock of sheep and some new geese and managed to persuade the person they'd sold Hector to to sell him back to them. Now, each morning Frank gets up and is really pleased when he can bring in an ordinary egg for Freda to cook on her own stove and for them both to share for their breakfast.

Interactive Follow-up

Questions

1) How did Frank and Freda feel about their life on the farm before the goose started laying the golden eggs? *(They were perfectly happy and enjoyed their life together.)*
2) How did Frank and Freda start acting differently when the eggs came? *(They began to buy new things, although they had actually been perfectly happy with the old things before: they even got rid of Hector the friendly pig.)*
3) How did Frank and Freda feel when the goose stopped laying the golden eggs? *(They were worried and angry, because they wanted more.)*
4) What happened to the goose? *(They killed the goose, because they thought she was keeping the eggs to herself, but they soon found out this was not so and they had killed her for nothing.)*

Getting the message

1) Frank and Freda had been happy before the golden eggs came. How did they get money to buy things for themselves? *(They earned it by working on their farm.)*
2) Why were they happy? *(Because they liked their life on the farm and they had all they needed.)*
3) How did the golden eggs change that? *(They suddenly thought that they needed newer, grander things and got rid of things that they had been happy with before. They also stopped doing the farm work and cooking etc that had made them happy before.)*

Learning more

1) Now, here's a hard question: Did having lots of money make Frank and Freda happier? Put your hand up if you think it did. Now put your hand up if it didn't. *(It actually made them more discontent, because they stopped being happy with their life and the things around them, and made them want to change things.)*
2) Do you think that they shouldn't have bought themselves ANY nice new things, then?

Non-interactive Follow-up

Summary

- Frank and Freda lived happily, working on their small farm.
- One of their geese started to lay golden eggs, and Frank and Freda were delighted to be so rich.
- They got rid of many things they had been happy with before and replaced them with smart new things.
- When the goose stopped laying the eggs, they became worried and then angry.
- They decided to kill the goose to get at the eggs inside her.
- There were no eggs inside the goose and they realised how foolish they had been.
- They learned their lesson and went back to being happy with what they had.

Reflection

Sometimes, when we see adverts for expensive things on television, we can get carried away and think that we can't be happy without them. Next time you feel like that, try to think of Frank and Freda: they found that having smart new things didn't actually make them feel any happier at all. Thankfully, they learned a big lesson and ended up being far happier again.

Prayer

Lord God, thank you that money can help us to buy the things that we need. Please help us to use our money wisely and not to think that having lots of money will always make us happy. Help us to be content with the things we have and to be generous to people who have less than us. Amen.

3A IMPROVING HEALTH: "LUNCH BOX"

Objective
To help children recognise that they can begin to make choices towards living a healthier lifestyle.

PSHE/Citizenship links
3a: how to make simple choices to improve their health and well-being.

Props
Two lunch boxes: one containing healthy fruit, salad vegetables and a sandwich, the other containing nothing but chocolate, sweets and crisps.

Introduction
We all need food to keep us healthy and to give us enough energy to get through each day. Today we've got two poems about the food we eat at dinnertime when we're at school. There's one about school dinners and one about packed lunches, so there's something for everyone. Listen carefully, because I'm going to ask you some questions about them afterwards.

POEM: "LUNCH BOX" BY JUDITH NICHOLS

Lunch boxes,
Munch boxes,
Pink, blue and red!
I've got cheese and apple
And thirteen loaves of bread!

Lunch boxes,
Munch boxes,
Yellow, white and blue!
I've got twenty sandwiches,
How about you?

Lunch boxes,
Munch boxes,
Brown, black and pink!
Mine is full of jelly beans
(At least that's what I *think!*)

Lunch boxes,
Munch boxes,
Purple, orange, green!
Mine is full of chocolate drops
And strawberry ice cream!

Lunch boxes,
Munch boxes,
Scarlet, emerald, grey!
Mine's a finger-licking secret...
What's in *yours* today?

[© Judith Nicholls 2007, reproduced by permission of the author.]

Interactive Follow-up

Questions

That poem was all about what goes into our lunch boxes. Who can remember what was in some of those lunch boxes? *(cheese, apple, sandwiches, jelly beans, chocolate drops, strawberry ice cream)* Well remembered!

The second poem is all about having school dinners and it goes like this:

Poem: "The Dinner-lady" by John Yeoman

The dinner-lady said to me,
"You're taking far too long.
You finish up that lovely cod:
It makes you big and strong."

The dinner-lady said to me,
"Those toffee bars aren't nice.
You finish up your shepherd's pie,
And then your prunes and rice."

The dinner-lady said to me,
"Those snacks you eat are trash.
You finish up your luncheon meat
And frozen peas and mash."

But, peering through the serving hatch,
I swear it made me blink,
I saw her with a bag of crisps
And tin of fizzy drink.

[Reproduced by permission of A P Watt Ltd on behalf of John Yeoman.]

Questions

1) What food was the dinner-lady trying to get the girl in the poem to eat?
   (fish, shepherd's pie, prunes, rice, meat, peas and mash)
2) What sorts of things did she complain about the girl eating?
   (toffee bars and trashy snacks)
3) Why do you think she wanted the girl to eat up her 'proper' food?
   (Because it's healthier and better for you than sweets and snacks.)
4) Grown ups find it just as hard as children do to resist unhealthy snacks – what happened to the dinner-lady at the end of the poem?
   (She is caught tucking in to crisps and fizzy drinks.)

Getting the message

(Ask for two volunteers to come to the front to open the two lunch boxes.)
I'd like you to open these lunch boxes and show everyone what's inside them, please. Take the things out one at a time, hold them up and tell us what they are.

Well done. Now, which lunchbox would you prefer to have, I wonder? Hands up who'd prefer this one *(holding up sweet-packed box)* and hands up who'd prefer this one *(hold up healthier option)*.

Now, most of us love chocolate and crisps and fizzy drinks, but did you know that too much of them isn't very good for us at all? If we have a lunchbox like this every day, we will soon get quite poorly. Having too many sweets and chocolates even makes some people behave badly, and makes them unable to sit quietly and do their school work. It's true, having too many sweet and snacks sometimes causes children to behave so badly that they end up being told off a lot.

Learning more

Does that mean that we should *never* have any chocolates and snacks with our lunch, then? No, of course not! There's nothing wrong with having them sometimes, as long as you usually eat plenty of healthy things like fruit, vegetables, bread and salads. Next time you get asked what you'd like in your lunchbox, make sure you ask for some juicy, crunchy fresh foods, instead of chocolate bars and crisps; and, if you stay for school dinners, make sure you tuck into the lovely healthy fresh food that the dinner-ladies prepare for you: you'll be amazed how much better you feel! What might you ask for, for your dinner tomorrow? *(Invite suggestions.)*

Non-interactive Follow-up

Summary

- A poem about the contents of lunch boxes, listing a variety of food items, some healthy and some less than healthy.
- A second poem about a dinner-lady who tries to encourage a girl to eat the healthy things she has cooked for the children, instead of eating unhealthy snacks.
- The dinner-lady doesn't practise what she preaches, however, and is caught tucking into crisps and fizzy drinks when she thinks no one is looking.

Reflection

If you really don't think you can do without chocolate and other snacks like that, what do you think you could do? One idea might be to ask for one chocolaty snack and one piece of fresh fruit – that way you get the best of both worlds! Remember, even if your mum has always put sweet snacks into your lunchbox, you can always ask her to give you some other things now instead: you can help yourself stay healthy by making that choice.

Prayer

Lord God, thank you that there are so many nice things for us to eat. Thank you that we can make choices in what we eat. Please help us to enjoy the things that are good for us, to keep us strong and healthy and help us not to eat too much of the things that aren't so good for us. Amen.

3B PERSONAL HYGIENE: WASH YOUR HANDS!

Objective
To help children understand the importance of maintaining personal hygiene.

PSHE/Citizenship links
3b: maintaining personal hygiene.

Props
None

Preparation
This assembly is in the form of an interactive rhyme which children can join in with. The first time it is read aloud, using version 1, the children can join in by saying the repeated line in italics. To underline the message and help children remember it, the second time it can be read using version 2, where the children have to complete the last word of each line. It may be a good idea to read version 1 twice, or to remind children of the words, before attempting version 2. A few mimed reminders will help for the missing words, although you might want to avoid miming the word loo!

Introduction
Today's assembly is all about keeping ourselves clean. Sometimes people get poorly because of germs they pick up from dirty objects and surfaces. To stop this from happening, there is a very simple thing that we all should do at least five or six times a day: washing our hands. To remind you when you should wash your hands, here's a rhyme, which you can join in with. After each line I say, you say, "Wash your hands!"

INTERACTIVE RHYME: WASH YOUR HANDS!

Version 1

If you go to the loo,
    Wash your hands!
And you're handling food too,
    Wash your hands!

If it gets to lunchtime,
    Wash your hands!
Or you're covered in grime,
    Wash your hands!

If you've been outdoors,
    Wash your hands!
Or you've touched the floor,
    Wash your hands!

Version 2

If you go to the . . . . ,
    Wash your hands!
And you're handling food . . . . ,
    Wash your hands!

If it gets to lunch. . . . . . . ,
    Wash your hands!
Or you're covered in . . . . ,
    Wash your hands!

If you've been out. . . . . . . ,
    Wash your hands!
Or you've touched the . . . . ,
    Wash your hands!

When there's paint on your mitts,
Wash your hands!
You have a bug or coughing fit,
Wash your hands!

At home and at school,
Wash your hands!
It's the golden rule,
Wash your hands!

When there's paint on your . . . . ,
Wash your hands!
You have a bug or coughing . . . . ,
Wash your hands!

At home and at . . . . ,
Wash your hands!
It's the golden . . . . ,
Wash your hands!

Interactive Follow-up

Questions

1) When should you wash your hands?
(The eight instances mentioned in the poem and more.)
2) Why do we need to wash our hands?
(They pick up bacteria or germs from dirty surfaces and these can get into our bodies, usually through the mouth, and make us ill. We can also pass on illnesses like colds this way.)
3) How should you wash your hands?
(With soap and warm water, if possible, washing both sides, but especially the fingers, and drying them afterwards with clean paper towels.)

Getting the message

1) What can happen to people who don't wash their hands? *(They can get diseases and conditions such as coughs, colds, viruses, stomach 'bugs', diarrhoea and worms, among many other things – and they will pass them all on.)*
2) Give these things a thumbs up, like this, if they are good ideas and a thumbs down, like this, if they are bad ideas:
   - Sucking your thumb.
   - Washing your hands before a meal.
   - Putting your fingers in your mouth.
   - Using soap when you have a wash.
   - Eating something that's been on the floor.

Learning more

What are bacteria? Why are they sometimes dangerous?

Non-interactive Follow-up

Summary

- You should wash your hands whenever you go to the toilet or handle food.
- You should also wash them before eating anything and if your hands look dirty.
- You should also wash them if you come in from outdoors and if you touch the floor.
- You should also wash them if you have paint, glue, clay or other art materials on them.
- You should also wash them regularly if you have a cold or a bug or a cough, to help stop it spreading.
- You should wash your hands at home and at school, and not just when you're told.

Reflection

Keeping your hands clean is good for lots of reasons – it can keep you healthy and stop germs from spreading. It's important that you remember to do it yourself without being told to do so all the time.

Prayer

Lord God, please help us to remember to wash our hands at all the times we should. Thank you that we have water and washbasins and soap and towels freely available when many people don't. Help us to make the most of them and to look after our bodies. Amen.

3c How diseases spread: Bobby Gough, the Boy with the Cough

Objective
To help children understand how some diseases spread and can be controlled.

PSHE/Citizenship links
3c: how diseases spread.

Props
None

Introduction
Today's assembly tells the story of a boy who had a nasty habit and how it spoiled his special day.

Poem: Bobby Gough, the Boy with the Cough

Once, a boy called Bobby Gough
Went to school with a terrible cough;
It tickled his throat and made him croak,
But the frog in his throat wasn't a joke.

Although Bobby himself didn't seem to care,
As he flopped himself down on his classroom chair.
He always had colds and coughs and sneezes
And sometimes more unpleasant diseases.

His classmates, though, were not so glad;
In fact, Bobby's coughing made them sad:
First of all the noise was grim,
But something far worse came from him.

You see, Bobby's mouth was open wide
When he coughed, and gunge inside
Came spraying out like bits of spit,
So everything around was hit.

"Bobby Gough – use your hand!"
His teacher made a clear demand.
"Yes, cover your mouth or germs will spread,"
The girl in front of Bobby said.

But Bobby didn't seem to care;
"Germs can't travel through the air,"
He muttered to himself that day,
Though he was wrong in every way.

Germs *can* travel through the air,
And that's just what they did right there;
From Bobby's mouth they spread around
To where his classmates all were found.

So the boys and girls of Bobby's school
Breathed in germs spread by a fool
Who couldn't be bothered to use his palm
To stop his friends from coming to harm.

Next school day, Bobby moved about
Giving birthday invitations out;
He was having a party, all could come,
He'd begged and pleaded with his mum.

One week later there were balloons on the door
At Bobby's house – number forty-four;
And inside, jelly, cakes and treats
Were piled high for his guests to eat.

"This'll be the best party ever,"
Said Bobby to his budgie, Trevor;
But 2 o'clock came with no knock on the door;
What were his friends all waiting for?

Then the phone rang, and again and again;
His mum came in saying, "That was Ben,
And Jon and Sue and lots of others,
Well, actually not them, their mothers."

"I'm sorry, Bobby, but no one can come."
"What!" he cried, "Not even one?"
"That's right," said Mum, "the party's off,
They're all in bed with nasty coughs."

Interactive Follow-up

Questions

1) What was Bobby Gough's nasty habit?
   (He didn't cover his mouth with his hand when he coughed.)
2) What happened at Bobby's birthday party?
   (No one came because all of his friends were in bed with coughs.)
3) How did all of Bobby's classmates get a cough?
   (They breathed in germs spread through the air when Bobby coughed.)

Getting the message

1) What can we learn from this poem?
2) You can stop yourself from catching coughs and colds in lots of ways. Call out the word which finishes off each sentence:
   - Before you eat, always wash your .... *(hands)*
   - Cover your mouth when you have a .... *(cough)*
   - Don't put your fingers in your .... *(mouth)*
   - If you have a cold, use a tissue to blow your .... *(nose)*
   - When you sneeze, turn away from other .... *(people)*

Non-interactive Follow-up

Summary

- Barry Gough went to school with a cough.
- He had lots of colds and viruses.
- He coughed on his classmates because he didn't cover his mouth with his hand.
- This made him unpopular and it spread germs through the air.
- Bobby invited his classmates to his birthday party.
- No one came to his party because all of his classmates were in bed with coughs.

Something to think about

Why do adults often tell children to use soap when they wash their hands?

Reflection

Try very hard not to spread coughs and viruses like colds. You can do this by washing your hands, using a tissue and covering your mouth and nose when you have to cough or sneeze. We can't always stop ourselves from catching diseases, but we can make it happen less often.

Prayer

Lord God, help us not to spread coughs and colds. Please help us to remember to cover our mouths when we cough and to wash our hands carefully. Thank you that we have medicines to make us better when we catch diseases and please keep us healthy and strong. Amen.

3D GROWING FROM YOUNG TO OLD: CHANGING NEEDS

Objective

To help children become aware of how people's needs change as they grow from young to old.

PSHE/Citizenship links

3d: growing older.

Props

This assembly needs quite a lot of preparation. The teacher will need to prepare 5 coloured cards, A3 or A4 in size, with the following ages written on them in large letters (one on each): 8 months, 8 years, 18 years, 38 years, 88 years. There will also need to be ten A3 or A4 pieces of white paper with the following written on them in large letters (in brackets are suggested illustrations which could be printed from clipart):

- Lots of sleep (a bed).
- Help with feeding (a spoon).
- Toys and books (a toy such as Lego and a book).
- School (a school or classroom scene).
- Learning to drive (a car with L-plate).
- Leaving home (a house).
- Family (a family with children).
- Job (an adult at a desk).
- Lots of rest (a comfy chair).
- Help with cooking (a saucepan).

Introduction

Every person in the world is different. No one is exactly the same as another person, not even twins. All of you have different lives. But there is one thing that happens to everybody, whoever they are. I wonder what it is – any ideas? *(Answer: growing older.)* Today's assembly is all about how you change and what you need as you grow older.

PRESENTATION: CHANGING NEEDS

First of all, I'd like five sensible volunteers up here at the front, please. *(5 children come to front.)* Now, let's pretend that these five children are all people of different ages. *(Pointing to first child.)* For this assembly, ... *(child's name)* is just 8 **months old** – a little baby *(give the child the '8 months' card to hold)*. Babies that age can't stand up by themselves, so you'd better sit.

(Pointing to second child.) For this assembly, ... *(child's name)* is going to be 8 **years old** – like a boy/girl in the juniors, a bit older than you *(give the child the '8 years' card to hold)*. You can certainly stand up by yourself.

(Pointing to third child.) Now, ... *(child's name)* is **18 years old** – a big grown up teenager *(give the child the '18 years' card to hold)*. Well done.

(Pointing to fourth child.) Now, ... *(child's name)* is **38 years old** – a person who has been an adult for quite a while *(give the child the '38 years' card to hold)*. That's it – act very grown up and sensible.

(Pointing to fifth child.) Now, finally, ... *(child's name)* is **88 years old** – someone very old: what we call an elderly person *(give the child the '88 years' card to hold)*. Perhaps we'd better give you a chair to sit on.

Now then, these five people are all different ages and they all need different things. Let's see if we can find out what they need...

(Mix up the white cards and hold them up one at a time. Ask the audience to match each card with one of the five age groups by giving it to them. The 5 volunteers should hold up the white cards, covering the coloured card with one if necessary).

So there we are, you can see that, as we grow older, we all need very different things. Let's give our five volunteers a clap.

Interactive Follow-up

Questions

1) What other things does a baby need?
(Love, clothes, changing nappy, sleep, etc.)
2) What other things does an 8 year old child need?
(More clothes, friends to play with, a bedroom, school things, etc.)
3) What other things does an 18 year old teenager need?
(Money, things for college or work, friends to talk to, mobile phone, etc.)
4) What other things does a 38 year old person need?
(A job, a home, maybe a partner, money, car, etc.)
5) What other things does an 88 year old person need?
(Company, help with cleaning, medical care, exercise, etc.)

Getting the message

1) How do people change as they get older? *(They become more independent – until they become very elderly – but also have to take on more responsibility.)*
2) There are some things that everybody needs. Show how important you think they are by giving each one a score with your fingers: 10 fingers = very important; 5 fingers = quite important; 1 finger = not important:
   - Somewhere to live.
   - Good food to eat.
   - Friends.
   - Love and attention.
   - Comfortable clothes.
   - Money.

Learning more

What's the best thing about being a grown up do you think?

NON-INTERACTIVE FOLLOW-UP

Summary

- Young babies need feeding and lots of sleep, amongst other things.
- 8 year olds need toys and school to learn, amongst other things.
- 18 year olds often need to leave home and learn to drive, amongst other things.
- People aged 38 often need to look after their family and to go to work, amongst other things.
- Elderly people of 88 need plenty of rest and help with tasks like cooking, amongst other things.

Something to think about

How should you treat elderly people that you meet?

Reflection

Everyone is different and everyone grows older. As we grow older, the things that we need change. Try to treat everyone you meet well, whatever age they are – think about how you like to be treated yourself.

Prayer

Lord God, thank you that we all change and grow up and have the chance to do new and exciting things as we get older. Please help us to treat everyone with kindness and respect, whatever age they are, and to think about their needs. Amen.

3F Household products: Too Much of a Good Thing

Objective

To help children learn that household products, including medicines, can be harmful if not used properly.

PSHE/Citizenship links

3f: household products.

Props

(Not essential): a medicine bottle

Introduction

There is a saying that 'you can have too much of a good thing'. One little girl certainly found out that this is true in today's story.

Story: Too Much of a Good Thing

Greer was a girl, oh, about the same age as you. She lived in Denmark, which is a country across the sea. She lived there a few years ago – I don't know if she's still there now. Maybe she is, maybe she's not.

When Greer was in the infants class at her little village school by the sea, there was one thing that she always wanted to do, one hope in her heart: that she would be chosen to play Mary in the Christmas nativity play. The school had performed this play for as long as anyone could remember, even Greer's grandpa, who was 77 years old. He sometimes sat with the other old men of the village by the big tree on the green and he told Greer that he played a shepherd in the nativity play when he was six. "Of course, the school was different then," he said. "It was in a little wooden hut, not a strong brick building like you have. But the Christmas play was just the same. And it always will be."

Greer's mother warned her not to be too disappointed if she didn't get to be Mary in the play. "There are lots of other good parts, Greer. You'd make a lovely angel."

"I was an angel last year," said Greer. "It was OK, but not as good as being Mary. Mary gets to ride on Mr Jensen's donkey."

It was true: the school used a real donkey in the play, provided by a kind local farmer. It made the play really special, although one year Greer's father told her that the donkey got nervous and tipped Mary off and made a mess outside the hall.

The following day, Mrs Sands, Greer's teacher, read out the names of all of the children and which parts they would have in the Nativity play. Greer was almost shaking with anticipation.

"Peter, you will be the innkeeper; Karrin, you will be the innkeeper's wife; Henning, you will be Joseph and Greer, you will play the part of Mary..." Greer nearly whooped with excitement. After school, she ran home instead of walking, tearing along the little lane to tell her mother the news. Unfortunately, because Greer was running so fast, she didn't see the patch of ice next to the barn. It had been very cold in the night and this piece of ground never thawed because it was always in shadow. Greer slipped and fell, catching her foot on a tree root as she tumbled. It didn't seem to hurt too much, though, and she was too excited to care.

In the bath that night, Greer was still babbling to her mother about playing Mary in the play. She wanted her costume to be just right and she had to go round to Mr Jensen's at the weekend to practise sitting on his old donkey. It was just as she mentioned the donkey that Greer's mum noticed the cut and bruise on her big toe.

"Oh, that's where I fell over in the lane today," said Greer. "It stings a bit." Her mother dried the toe carefully when Greer was out of the bath and put a plaster on it. She noticed that Greer was hobbling a little as she went down the stairs.

A week later, rehearsals for the school nativity play were in full swing. But there was just one problem: Greer wasn't there. She was home in bed, ordered to stay there by her doctor. Greer had been hobbling on her foot for a few days and had started to complain about feeling strange too. She had lost her appetite and gone very pale.

"I'm afraid Greer has an infection in her toe," said Doctor Brandt to her mother. "It's nothing serious, so don't worry. It'll take a few days to get better, but she will need to take some medicine." Greer's mother stroked her daughter's hair.

"But the nativity play is in a week's time," said Greer. "Will I still be able to play Mary? I do hope so." She sounded so worried. Her mother looked at the doctor for an answer.

"I would say that you have a good chance of being completely better in a week," he said. "But you must stay in bed and rest, and take the medicine." Greer looked more hopeful.

"I'll be able to learn my lines in bed."

Her mother smiled, "Well, just for a few minutes each day."

Four days later, Greer was feeling a little better. Some colour had returned to her cheeks and she was now eating again. She had learned all of her lines for the part of Mary and had spent ages nagging her mother to phone her teacher, Mrs Sands, at school to tell her that she would be alright to be in the play.

"Well, perhaps I will now that you're eating again," said her mother. "That medicine certainly seems to have done the trick. But I can't tell Mrs Sands that you'll definitely be alright for the play, Greer – we still don't know that yet. I'll just say probably."

Greer grumbled but it was no use arguing. Her mother disappeared to go to the telephone and Greer got up to walk to the toilet.

While she was in the bathroom, Greer noticed a small brown bottle. It was the thick yellow medicine that she had been taking to make her toe better. The white plastic spoon was next to it. Greer heard her mother's voice in the hall downstairs – she was talking to Mrs Sands on the phone. Greer picked up the bottle and she had an idea. What if she took some more medicine? She'd already had a spoonful at lunchtime with her meal but surely, she thought to herself, if she took some more now she would get better more quickly and she would definitely be well enough to play Mary at the nativity.

She twisted the lid of the bottle and it came off easily – her mother hadn't tightened it properly. She looked at the spoon but decided it would be easier to just drink it from the bottle. Greer tipped the bottle to her lips and put her head back. Nothing came at first but then a thick gloop of the sticky medicine poured into her open mouth, almost causing her to choke. She put the bottle down and took a drink of water from the tap. She put the lid of the bottle back on and hurried back to her bed, just as her mother put the phone down and came up the stairs.

Later that day, Greer was sick. She had a terrible pain in her stomach and her mother called Doctor Brandt because she was so worried. He took her temperature and looked at her carefully. "Where is Greer's medicine?" he asked. Greer's mother went to get the bottle from the bathroom and handed it to the doctor. He weighed it in his hands then took off the lid and looked inside. "Has Greer been taking one spoonful a day, as directed?" he asked. Her mother nodded, then the doctor looked at Greer. She could tell that he knew what had happened.

Greer was sick for two days, but even when she felt better on the third day, she was told that she would have to stay in bed. She would have to miss the nativity play: someone else would sit on the donkey that year. Greer cried when her mother told her that Mrs Sands had asked her friend Leena to play the part of Mary. He mother stroked her hair but there was really nothing to say.

Interactive Follow-up

Questions

1) Why was the story called 'Too Much of a Good Thing'?
   (Because Greer had too much medicine and it made her ill, so that she missed out on the nativity play.)
2) How did Greer get poorly at first?
   (She hurt her toe when she slipped on some ice and fell over.)
3) Why did Greer cry at the end?
   (She had set her heart on playing Mary in the nativity, but missed it because she was not well.)

Getting the message

1) Why is medicine usually in bottles with special child-proof lids? *(Because medicine can be harmful if too much is taken.)*
2) Medicines come in many types. Say yes or no if each of these can be a medicine:
   - Tablets
   - Plasters
   - Paper
   - Bandages
   - Pills
   - Liquid
   - A cream
   - A powder

Learning more

Apart from medicines, what other things found in most houses can be harmful? *(Parents' alcohol, household cleaning chemicals and sharp things such as knives, etc.)*

NON-INTERACTIVE FOLLOW-UP

Summary

- Greer was a young girl living in Denmark.
- She wanted to play the part of Mary in the school nativity play and to ride a real donkey.
- She was given the part of Mary but she fell over when running home with the news.
- Her toe was injured and she became poorly, so her doctor gave her some medicine.
- Greer was worried about being well enough for the play, so she drank extra medicine without asking or telling her mother.
- The medicine made her sick and so she missed the nativity play.

Something to think about

How can you tell if a household product such as a cleaner is dangerous or not?

Reflection

Remember that medicines can be harmful if not taken properly. They can make us better, but only if we follow the instructions and only take medicines that the doctor has given to us. Taking medicine that is meant for someone else is very dangerous. Look out for warning labels on dangerous household products like bleach and glue.

Prayer

Lord God, thank you that we have medicines which can make us better when we are poorly. Help us to be very careful with them and to use them properly. Please keep all of us safe. Amen.

3G RULES FOR KEEPING SAFE: PETER AND THE WOLF

Objective

To learn that many rules we don't understand or agree with are actually there to keep us safe and that it is important to stick to rules about safety.

PSHE/Citizenship links

3g: rules for, and ways of, keeping safe.

Props

None

Introduction

Do you get a bit fed up sometimes, when the grown ups around you keep going on about rules – things that you *must* do to keep yourself safe and things that you *mustn't* do to keep yourself safe. Today's story is about a boy who knew exactly what the rules were, but didn't want to follow them because he thought he knew better.

BOOK EXTRACT: *PETER AND THE WOLF* RETOLD BY IAN BECK

Early one morning, Peter opened the gate and walked out into the big green meadow. On a branch of a big tree sat a little bird, Peter's friend. "All is quiet," chirped the bird happily. Just then a duck came waddling round. She was glad that Peter had not closed the gate and decided to take a nice swim in the deep pond in the meadow. Seeing the duck, the little bird flew down upon on the grass, settled next to her and shrugged his shoulders.

"What kind of bird are you if you can't fly?" said he. To this the duck replied "What kind of bird are you if you can't swim?" and dived into the pond. They argued and argued, the duck swimming in the pond and the little bird hopping along the shore.

Suddenly, something caught Peter's attention. He noticed a cat crawling through the grass. The cat thought; "That little bird is busy arguing, I'll just grab him." Stealthily, the cat crept towards him on her velvet paws.

"Look out!" shouted Peter and the bird immediately flew up into the tree, while the duck quacked angrily at the cat, from the middle of the pond. The cat walked around the tree and thought, "Is it worth climbing up so high? By the time I get there the bird will have flown away."

Just then Grandfather came out. He was upset because Peter had gone in the meadow. "It's a dangerous place. If a wolf should come out of the forest, then what would you do?" But Peter paid no attention to his grandfather's words. Boys like him are not afraid of wolves. But Grandfather took Peter by the hand, led him home and locked the gate.

No sooner had Peter gone, than a big grey wolf came out of the forest. In a twinkling the cat climbed up the tree. The duck quacked, and in her excitement jumped out of the pond. But no matter how hard the duck tried to run, she couldn't escape the wolf. He was getting nearer, nearer, catching up with her. Then he got her, and with one gulp, swallowed her.

And now, this is how things stood: the cat was sitting on one branch, the bird on another… not too close to the cat. And the wolf walked around and around the tree, looking at them with greedy eyes.

In the meantime, Peter, without the slightest fear, stood behind the closed gate watching all that was going on. He ran home, got a strong rope, and climbed up the high stone wall. One of the branches of the tree, around which the wolf was walking, stretched out over the wall. Grabbing hold of the branch, Peter lightly climbed over on to the tree.

Peter said to the bird: "Fly down and circle over the wolf's head. Only take care that he doesn't catch you." The bird almost touched the wolf's head with his wings while the wolf snapped angrily at him, from this side and that. How the bird worried the wolf! How he wanted to catch him! But the bird was clever, and the wolf simply couldn't do anything about it.

Meanwhile, Peter made a lasso and carefully letting it down, caught the wolf by the tail and pulled with all his might. Feeling himself caught, the wolf began to jump wildly trying to get loose. But Peter tied the other end of rope to the tree, and the wolf's jumping only made the rope around his tail tighter.

Just then, the hunters came out of the woods, following the wolf's trail and shooting as they went. But Peter, sitting in the tree, said: "Don't shoot! Birdie and I have already caught the wolf. Now help us take him to the zoo." And now, imagine the triumphant procession: Peter at the head; after him the hunters leading the wolf; and winding up the procession, Grandfather and the cat.

Grandfather shook his head discontentedly: "Well, and if Peter hadn't caught the wolf? What then?" Above them flew Birdie chirping merrily.

"My, what brave fellows we are, Peter and I! Look what we have caught!" And if you listened very carefully, you could hear the duck quacking inside the wolf; because the wolf in his hurry, had swallowed her alive.

Interactive Follow-up

Questions

1) Where did Peter and his grandfather live?
   (By a green meadow at the edge of a big forest.)
2) What friend did Peter have? *(A bird.)*
3) What dangerous animal came out of the forest? *(A hungry wolf.)*
4) What terrible thing happened to the duck? *(She got swallowed whole.)*
5) How did the story end?
   (Peter caught the wolf and the hunters helped him take the wolf to the zoo.)

Getting the message

1) In the middle of the story, Peter's grandfather came out and was cross with Peter, because he'd broken an important rule. Here are some rules he might have broken – which one do you think it was?
   - Don't play with the animals.
   - Don't tease the cat.
   - Don't go into the meadow. (✓)
   - Don't eat ducks.
2) Why did Grandfather have the rule about not going into the meadow? *(Because it would be dangerous if a wolf came out of the forest.)*
3) Peter didn't think it was a good rule, because he wasn't afraid of wolves, but what do you think – was it a good rule? *(Open ended, but ask the children to consider that adults may often be more aware of danger and understand the seriousness of danger more fully than children. It's easy not to be scared, if you don't really understand the danger you might be in.)*

Learning more

Peter and the Wolf is a famous fairy tale and is all about Peter being a brave hero. In real life, though, a small boy couldn't really catch a wolf like that and the story can be a warning to make sure that we all stick to rules that are there to keep us safe. Here are some rules: give them a thumbs up, like this, if you think they are useful safety rules and a thumbs down, like this, if you don't:

- Never cross a road on your own.
- Never eat jelly on Tuesdays.
- Never get into a car or go off with someone you don't know.
- Never go off with anyone without telling your parents where you are going.
- Never try to catch a wolf on your own.
  (A good rule in theory, but not too relevant here!)

Non-interactive Follow-up

Summary

- Peter went out into the meadow, followed by the duck, the cat and the bird.
- The cat nearly caught the bird while the bird and the duck were arguing.
- Grandfather was cross with Peter for having broken the rule about going out into the meadow, and took him back home.
- A wolf came out of the forest and swallowed the duck whole.
- Peter, helped by the bird, caught the wolf with a rope.
- The hunters arrived and they all took the wolf to the zoo.
- They could still hear the duck quacking inside the wolf.

Reflection

Grandfather made the rule about not going into the meadow and keeping the gate shut to keep Peter safe. Peter broke the rule and put himself in danger, but he also put the duck in danger. Even though Peter was lucky, the story didn't end happily for the duck, because she got eaten. Whose fault was that, do you think: Peter's, the bird's, the cat's, the wolf's or even the duck's own fault?

Prayer

Lord God, thank you that we have rules that are there to help keep us safe. Sometimes it's hard to obey the ones that we don't really understand or don't agree with. Please help us to learn the important rules and to stick to them, so that we can stay safe. Amen.

4a How our behaviour affects others: One Thing Leads to Another

Objective
To raise awareness that our behaviour affects other people in both positive and negative ways.

PSHE/Citizenship links
4a: to recognise how their behaviour affects other people.

Props
(Not essential): a picture of a windmill

Introduction
Has anyone ever done something to you that you thought was a bit mean? It's not a nice feeling, is it? What did it make you feel like? This story is about a brother and sister who had some trouble getting on and who did some pretty mean things to each other.

Story: One Thing Leads to Another

The model stood on the table. It was a beautiful red and white striped windmill, with huge white sails that really went round and a little door at the bottom that really opened. Molly had been working on it ever since she'd seen a picture of a windmill in a book at school and thought it was the most beautiful thing she'd ever seen. Dad had had to help her, of course, because she wanted to make one with sails that really went round, and they'd finally finished it yesterday. It had taken a long time to make.

Even though she was so pleased with her windmill, Molly was pretty grumpy. Her twin brother Jack had borrowed her best book without asking and he'd lost it at school. He didn't even seem that sorry and she thought that was mean. To show him just how mean she thought it was, she'd gone into his bedroom and 'untidied' it a bit for him, tipping his things all over the floor. That'd show him! She felt a lot better and went down to the kitchen for a drink. She bumped shoulders with Jack as he pushed past her to go up the stairs.

"You horrid girl!" came Jack's voice – he'd only reached the top of the stairs but he could already see the mess Molly had made of his bedroom. In two seconds he'd thundered back down the stairs. He rushed over to where Molly was standing by the sink getting her drink and grabbed her ponytail. He pulled hard at her hair and then pushed her over. Molly kicked Jack as hard as she could from where she was now lying, and Mum had to pick them both up and separate them from each other. She looked VERY cross with them both. As she grabbed them, her arm brushed something big that was standing on the table…

CRASH! Molly and Jack both jumped, as they heard the loud thump behind them. Oh no – it was the windmill! Molly had left it there on the kitchen table, so that everyone could see it, and now it lay in pieces on the floor.

Everything went completely quiet as they all stared at the broken model. Then Molly burst into tears and ran out before her mum could stop her. She went and hid in her bedroom and cried and cried. Jack just stayed where he was, looking at the windmill. He watched Mum pick it up carefully and put the pieces onto the table. She didn't look cross any more – just sad.

"Now look what's happened!" sighed Mum. "I do wish that you two would be nicer to each other, instead of arguing and fighting so much."

"Oh Mum," said Jack, with a little quiver in his voice. "Molly and Dad spent AGES making that. She wanted to take it into school tomorrow to show it to her class." Suddenly he didn't feel cross any more either. He just felt sorry that something so important to Molly had got broken – and it was at least partly his fault. "Do you think that Dad will help me try and mend it?"

"I'm sure he will," said Mum, with a smile. "But you need to do something else, too – both of you."

"What's that, then?" asked Jack.

"Have a think about it and I'm sure that you'll know. Remember – it's something BOTH of you need to do."

Interactive Follow-up

Questions

1) What started everything off?
   (Molly was already grumpy because Jack had lost her favourite book at school and didn't seem sorry.)
2) What did Molly do? *(She messed up Jack's room because she was grumpy with him.)*
3) What happened next?
   (When Jack saw the mess, he ran back downstairs, pulled Molly's hair and pushed her over.)
4) What was the last, really bad thing that happened?
   (Mum was trying to stop them fighting when her arm caught the windmill and knocked it off the table. The windmill broke.)
5) Why was the windmill so precious? *(Because it had taken Dad and Molly so long to make it.)*
6) What do you think the mystery thing was that both Jack and Molly needed to do?
   (They needed to say sorry to each other – and really mean it. Remember, the thing that had really upset Molly about her book was that Jack hadn't seemed particularly sorry that he'd lost it.)

Getting the message

(Ask for three volunteers to come and stand at the front and represent the characters in the story.) Each of these people, Molly, Jack and Mum, were affected by what the others did to them. Let's see if we can find out how. Hands up if you can tell me:

- Molly *(She was cross that Jack had lost her book and wasn't sorry; Jack also pulled her hair and pushed her over.)*
- Jack *(He was angry that Molly had messed up his room on purpose.)*
- Mum *(She was cross that they were fighting and then sad because their behaviour had led to the windmill breaking.)*

Learning more

1) Although their behaviour did affect other people in a bad way in the story, Jack did something that affected the other characters in a good way, too. What did he do? *(He realised how important the windmill was to Molly (and probably Dad too) and offered to try to mend it. That pleased Mum and it would have pleased Molly too, when she heard about it.)*
2) What do you think the thing was that Mum meant Jack and Molly both needed to do? *(They both needed to say sorry to each other, instead of carrying on doing bad things to each other.)*

Non-interactive Follow-up

Summary of the assembly

- Molly and Dad had spent a long time making a model of a windmill together.
- Molly was grumpy because Jack had lost her favourite book at school and wasn't sorry.
- She messed up his room.
- Jack saw the mess, pulled Molly's hair and pushed her over.
- Mum tried to sop them fighting and knocked over the windmill as she tried to grab them.
- Molly ran off in tears and Jack offered to try to mend the windmill.
- Mum was pleased, but said that there was something else that both Jack and Molly needed to do.

Reflection

All of us sometimes do things that affect other people badly. When we realise that we have behaved in a way that has made someone else sad or cross, it's very important to say that we're sorry – and to really mean it. It's not always easy to do, but usually it's the only way to stop one bad thing leading to another, like with Jack and Molly.

Prayer

Lord God, thank you that we can make other people happy by saying and doing kind things. Please help us not to say and do things that will affect other people in a bad way – even people we don't much like. If we have affected someone by our bad behaviour, please make us brave enough to say sorry and try to put things right. Amen.

4B LISTENING TO OTHERS: DAME TANNI

Objective
To help children appreciate the value of listening to others and co-operating.

PSHE/Citizenship links
4b: listening to others.

Props
(Not essential): a picture of Tanni Grey-Thompson, preferably in her race wheelchair

Preparation
This assembly is written in a play script format and requires four volunteer children to read a part: two girls (A and B) and two boys (C and D). The ideal presenters would be four good readers from Y6 with strong, clear voices. A short practice before the assembly would be very helpful, and each child will need a copy of the script.

Introduction
If you want to become very good at something, it's almost impossible do it on your own. You must learn to work with other people and to listen to what they say. If you do that, you can achieve all sorts, even if you have a difficult start in life, as today's true story shows.

TRUE STORY: DAME TANNI

One of Britain's most successful and well known athletes is Tanni Grey-Thompson. Tanni is a disabled athlete who has competed in the Paralympic games many times, representing her country. In total, she has won 11 gold medals.

Tanni was born with a medical condition called spinal bifida, which meant that she couldn't use her legs, and from the age of seven she has needed a wheelchair to move around. Despite her disability, Tanni always loved sport and she hoped one day to be really good at it. The sport she liked most when she was younger was basketball. Basketball is a game which many wheelchair users play but Tanni found she just wasn't any good at it.

After that, Tanni tried lots of sports but it wasn't until she was a teenager that she discovered athletics. Tanni had a go at a wheelchair race and found out that she did really well. She had a go in a special lightweight wheelchair designed for racing and she loved it – she knew what she wanted to do from then on.

Tanni joined an athletics club and began to train so that she could get better and faster at racing. Training means that you have to work hard at practising something: doing it again and again until you are good and then practising even more until you are better. Tanni got to know a lot of other disabled teenagers who were good at sport but many of them left the club because they didn't want to train.

Sports training isn't something you always do alone. Most of the time you train with other athletes and also with a coach. A coach is a person who knows a lot about the sport and can help to make you better at it. Coaches usually make athletes work very hard because they know that that is the only way they will improve and win races. It would have been easy for Tanni to give up her sport as a girl, and instead concentrate on her social life or just stay at home and watch TV, but she wanted to achieve something special.

Tanni was good at racing, but to become *very* good she had to work together with her coach and the other athletes. She had to listen to the coach too: what to eat, when to get up, how many hours to practice, which distances to try, how much to drink, what to wear… the list went on and on. But Tanni was determined to do well: she listened and she worked with the other athletes to make herself better at racing.

It worked: when she was just 15 years old, Tanni represented Wales in the Junior National Championships, racing against other disabled athletes. Then, when she was just 19, she had the thrill of her life. She was chosen to represent Great Britain at the Paralympics in Korea, across the other side of the world. She travelled along with all the famous Olympic athletes and, when she competed, she won her first big medal: a bronze for finishing third in the 400m.

But that was only the beginning for Tanni: four years later she travelled with the British team to the 1992 Paralympics in Barcelona, where she won four gold medals. She also broke the world record in the 100m and 400m. Tanni was the best female wheelchair sprinter in the whole world! All the work she had done with her training partners had paid off.

The Sydney Paralympics of 2000 were very special for Tanni: she won gold medals in four races: the 100m, 200m, 400m and 800m. The last one was quite a long distance and Tanni knew then that she was able to win long races too. She entered a London Marathon and won. Since then, Tanni has won an incredible six London Marathons.

Three times Tanni has been given special awards by the Queen at Buckingham Palace to recognise her amazing achievements. In 2005, she was given a special title and is now known as Dame Tanni Grey-Thompson.

Recently, a reporter asked Tanni if having a dream of success is important. This is what she replied: "My grandfather always used to say to me: 'Aim high, even if you only hit a cabbage.' I think that's about having a goal and a dream, and just seeing what you might achieve, because unless you try you're never going to know what you're able to do."

Well, it's a good job that Tanni listened to him, isn't it?

Interactive Follow-up

Questions

1) Why does Tanni need to use a wheelchair?
   (She has spinal bifida, which means that she cannot use her legs.)
2) Why is Tanni famous? *(She has won 11 Paralympics gold medals plus many other awards.)*
3) What sport does Tanni do? *(Athletics: she races in her wheelchair.)*

Getting the message

1) Tanni's grandfather said "aim high": what did he mean by that?
2) Tanni succeeded because she worked with others and listened to them. Who do you think helped her the most? Vote for one of these people by putting up your hand:
   - Her friends.
   - Her athletics coach.
   - Her grandfather.
   - The other athletes.
   - Her family.

Non-interactive Follow-up

Summary

- Tanni Grey-Thompson is one of Britain's most famous athletes, despite being disabled.
- She has won 11 gold medals for wheelchair races at the Paralympics.
- She has spinal bifida, which means that she cannot use her legs.
- Tanni wanted to be a basketball player when she grew up.
- She discovered that she was better at racing and so she took up athletics.
- She trained hard, working together with a coach and other athletes.
- She won lots of medals and broke world records; she has won 6 London marathons.
- Tanni's grandfather gave her the advice to "aim high", meaning that you will only find out if you can do something really well by trying.

Something to think about

It's good to listen to other people: if you don't listen, how will people treat you?

Reflection

We can all learn from the amazing true life story of Tanni Grey-Thompson: we can learn to listen to others, work together with people and to aim high in life. If you do all these things, who knows what you might achieve?

Prayer

Lord God, help me to be a good listener, like Tanni Grey-Thompson. Help me to learn to work together to do things, like she did too. Thank you that she is a great example to us all. Amen.

4c Respecting differences: Frederick

Objective

To make children aware that people have different ways in which they contribute to society.

PSHE/Citizenship links

4c: to identify and respect the differences and similarities between people.

Props

(Not essential): Beanie Baby type toy mouse, some ears or grains of wheat and a bunch of flowers, or large projected picture of a mouse.

Introduction

Do you sometimes feel that you work harder than some of your friends, if there's a job that you all have to work on together? Today's story, by Leo Lionni, is about a family of mice who all had to work very hard to get enough supplies to help them through the winter. But one of the mice didn't seem to understand that he needed to join in and help out too...

Book extract: *Frederick* by Leo Lionni

All along the meadow where the cows grazed and the horses ran, there was an old stone wall. In that wall, not far from the barn and the granary, a chatty family of field mice had their home. But the farmers had moved away, the barn was abandoned and the granary stood empty. And since winter was not far off, the little mice began to gather corn and nuts and wheat and straw. They all worked day and night. All – except Frederick.

"Frederick, why don't you work?" they asked.

"I do work," said Frederick. "I gather sun rays for the cold dark winter days."

And when they saw Frederick sitting there, staring at the meadow, they said: "And now, Frederick?"

"I gather colours," answered Frederick simply. "For winter is grey."

And once Frederick seemed half asleep. "Are you dreaming, Frederick?" they asked reproachfully.

But Frederick said, "Oh no, I am gathering words. For the winter days are long and many, and we'll run out of things to say."

The winter days came, and when the first snow fell the five little mice took to their hideout in the stones. In the beginning there was lots to eat, and the mice told stories of foolish foxes and silly cats. They were a happy family. But little by little they had nibbled up most of the nuts and berries, the straw was gone and the corn was only a memory. It was cold in the wall and no one felt like chatting. Then they remembered what Frederick had said about sun rays and colours and words.

"What about your supplies, Frederick?" they asked.

"Close your eyes," said Frederick, as he climbed on a big stone. "Now I send you the rays of the sun. Do you feel how their golden glow..." And, as Frederick spoke of the sun, the four little mice began to feel warmer. Was it Frederick's voice? Was it magic?

"And how about the colours, Frederick?" they asked anxiously.

"Close your eyes again," Frederick said. And when he told them of the blue periwinkles and the red poppies in the yellow wheat, and the green leaves of the berry bush, they saw the colours as clearly as if they had been painted in their minds.

"And the words, Frederick?"

Frederick cleared his throat, waited a moment, and then, as if from a stage, he said:
"Who scatters snowflakes? Who melts the ice?
Who spoils the weather? Who makes it nice?
Who grows the four-leaf clovers in June?
Who dims the daylight? Who lights the moon?

Four little field mice who live in the sky.
Four little field mice... like you and I.

One is the Springmouse who turns on the showers.
Then comes the Summer who paints in the flowers.
The Fallmouse is next with walnuts and wheat.
And Winter is last... with little cold feet.

Aren't we lucky the seasons are four?
Think of a year with one less... or one more!"

When Frederick had finished, they all applauded. "But Frederick," they said, '"you are a poet!"

Frederick blushed, took a bow, and said shyly, "I know it."

Interactive Follow-up

Questions

1) Where did the field mice live?
   (In a hole in a stone wall near an old abandoned farm.)
2) Why did they need to collect so much food?
   (Because winter was coming and they needed to build up their stores.)
3) Did the whole family join in with the hard work?
   (No – Frederick didn't seem to be doing anything to help.)
4) What did Frederick have to say when they said he wasn't working?
   (He said he was working – he was collecting the sun's rays, and colours and words for the long, cold grey winter.)

Getting the message

If you had been one of the other mice, would you have let Frederick share the food you'd worked so hard to collect, I wonder? Put your hand up if you would. Why? *(Ask one or two children.)* Now put your hand up if you wouldn't share your food with him, because he hadn't helped collect any. *(Again ask one or two children to say why they wouldn't.)*

In the end, Frederick proved that he did have something to share with the other mice – what was that? *(He shared his memories of warm summer days and bright flowers, and helped them feel better by giving them things to remember and imagine, to make the long cold days and nights seem warmer and brighter.)*

Learning more

We aren't all good at the same things: I'm going to mention just some things that you could be good at. Put your hands up when you hear something that you're really good at: *(pause between each, to give them time to consider and put their hands up)*

- Sport
- Painting and drawing
- Helping at home
- Dancing
- Reading
- Sewing
- Number work
- Writing
- Being friendly

We are all good at different things and no one can possibly be good at every single thing there is to do – we're all different and that's a good thing.

Non-interactive Follow-up

Summary

- Five field mice lived in an old stone wall near an abandoned farm.
- As winter approached, they all worked hard to collect food – all except Frederick.
- The others thought he wasn't working hard like them.
- He said that he was working hard at collecting sun rays and colours and words to help them through the long, dark winter days.
- When winter came, all the mice shared the food they'd collected.
- When it began to run out, and they ran out of things to talk about, they asked Frederick to share the things he'd collected.
- He told them about the warmth of the sun and beautiful colours, and told them poems about the seasons, and they all felt better.
- The other mice suddenly understood that what Frederick had to share was just as important as their food had been.

Reflection

Just imagine how boring and dreary it would have been for the family of mice if Frederick had been like all the others and just collected food, and hadn't been able to share his memories with them when things got cold and dark. But also think how bad it would have been if all five mice had been poets like Frederick: there would have been plenty of lovely words, but no food at all. It's good that we are all good at different things.

Prayer

Lord God, thank you that we are all so different. Please help us to understand that none of us can be good at *everything* we try to do. Help us not to show off about the things that we find easy, and to be pleased when people can help us out with things that we're not so good at. Amen.

4D Caring for each other: Jack and Nina

Objective

To help children learn that family and friends should care for each other.

PSHE/Citizenship links

4d: caring for each other.

Props

None

Introduction

It's nice when someone cares about us, isn't it? It's good when people give us presents or say kind things or when we get a hug from someone in our family. But it's no good just being someone who receives care from other people; we need to give care too. Today's assembly is a true story about two people who are a wonderful example of how we should care for each other.

True Story: Jack and Nina

Jack and Nina were brother and sister. Jack was much older than Nina – in fact he was eight years old when she was born. Jack was excited about having a baby sister and helped to look after her from the start, helping to feed her and to cuddle her and even to change her nappy.

When Nina was a naughty toddler, Jack used to spend ages playing with her, building towers out of wooden bricks and helping to dress her teddies in daft clothes. Nina loved Jack and Jack loved Nina.

By the time that Nina was old enough to go to school, Jack was a big teenager and he didn't see so much of her, but the two of them were always close when they were together, sharing books and jokes and running around the garden playing hide and seek. By the time Nina was aged eleven and in her final year at primary school, Jack had left home and gone to be a student at university. Nina was sad when Jack went but she spoke to him on the phone a lot and sent him emails and texts every week.

It was round about this time that Nina became poorly. At first she just complained of feeling tired after school, but soon she stopped eating and went very pale. She had no energy at all. The doctor wasn't sure what it was: she had no spots or anything else on the outside. He said that she should stay at home in bed for a while to see what happened. Nina did that but, instead of getting better, she grew worse. She was full of aches and pains and she could hardly even swallow, never mind eat anything. She was so weak that she could hardly stand up to walk. Her parents were very worried and called the doctor again. He said that she should be taken to hospital right away.

When Jack heard that Nina was in hospital, he caught the first train from university and came home right away. He then got a lift to the hospital, where Nina was delighted to see him, even though she hardly had the energy to lift her head and smile. Jack was shocked to see how pale and thin his sister looked. He stayed with her in the hospital for hours, chatting and, when she was too tired to talk, just keeping her company. Nina was so glad that her big brother was there, especially as she had to keep having medical tests to find out what was the matter with her.

When Nina was asleep, Jack went home, but he came back to the hospital the next day and he brought Nina a special surprise: it was her favourite cuddly toy, a little penguin called Ping. Nina was very excited to have Ping with her in the hospital and she cuddled him all day while she sat with Jack. She also managed to swallow some of the special sticky drink that the nurses gave her instead of food.

A few days later, a doctor from the hospital came to see Nina and her parents and Jack. He said that Nina had had lots of tests and she didn't have any of the serious diseases that the doctors thought her illness might be. They still weren't sure what she did have but they would keep her in hospital until she was eating again and had enough energy to walk. In the meanwhile, they would get her a wheelchair to move about in. Nina liked the wheelchair: it was a shiny new purple one with patterns on it, and she really enjoyed being pushed about in the hospital ward, especially by Jack.

Jack stayed a few more days and then went back to university because he had work to do. After three weeks in hospital, Nina felt quite a lot better. She had started eating again and could sit up and even walk a little bit, although she still needed her wheelchair to get to the toilet. The doctors said they thought she had something called fibromyalgia. They didn't have any medicine to make it better but they thought that Nina was well enough to go home, even though she wouldn't be able to go back to school for a while.

Nina and Jack kept in touch as much as they could over the next few weeks. Then, one day, Jack phoned from university to say that he didn't feel well. In fact, he thought he was getting the same illness that Nina had. He went to see his doctor. It was true, Jack had fibromyalgia too. He became very tired and felt rotten most of the time. He came home for a long rest. The good news was that he didn't have the illness as badly as Nina: he was eating alright and he didn't need a wheelchair to move around.

After a good rest, Jack was able to go back to university, even though he was still a little poorly. Nina stayed at home where, very slowly, she began to get better too. After a year, she was able to go to her new school for a few hours: that was very exciting but very tiring too. Some days she had no energy but on other days she felt quite well.

Far away at university, Jack was the same – he just about managed his work but he needed lots of rest. When he had a bad day, he talked on the phone to Nina. She understood exactly how he felt and she was able to cheer him up a lot. It really helped having a sister like her who really cared. And, when Nina was having a bad spell with the illness, Jack called her and did his best to make her smile and laugh. They were very good for each other and, when Jack came home from the holidays, they always greeted each other with a big hug.

Jack and Nina are a little older now. They still have the illness but both of them are getting better a little bit at a time. They both long for the day when they'll be fully well again but, for now, they're just glad that they have each other.

INTERACTIVE FOLLOW-UP

Questions

1. How old was Jack when Nina was a little baby? *(Eight)*
2. What sort of things did they used to do together as they grew up?
   (Played, talked, emailed, spent time with each other.)
3. What happened to Nina and Jack?
   (They both became ill with fibromyalgia: first Nina, who went to hospital, then Jack who was at university.)
4. How did they care for each other when they became ill?
   (They phoned each other and talked, cheering each other up; Jack also visited Nina in hospital when she was first poorly.)

Getting the message

1) Why was Nina so glad to see Jack when she was in hospital? *(Because he was far away and she was feeling sad and miserable; she didn't expect to see him; it was a surprise; he cheered her up; he really cared about her.)*
2) You can show that you care for others in lots of different ways. Give each of these a score for how good they are: one thumb up for good or two thumbs up for very good:
   - Saying a kind word to someone.
   - Thanking a person for something they have done.
   - Giving a person a present.
   - Spending time talking to someone.
   - Doing a job for a person that needs doing.
   - Smiling.
   - Helping someone who needs help.

Learning more

Sometimes you can show that you care for someone just by listening to them: do you agree?

Non-interactive Follow-up

Summary of the assembly

- Jack and Nina were brother and sister.
- Jack was eight years older than Nina and he helped care for her as a baby.
- Jack played with Nina when she was a toddler and when she was at school: they loved each other.
- When she was 11, Nina became ill and had to go to hospital; Jack came home from university to visit her, which helped her a lot.
- Jack became poorly with the same illness and Nina helped him by cheering him up on the phone.
- They both still have fibromyalgia but they care for each other and help each other with the illness.

Something to think about

Being helpful shows that you care: how can you be helpful at home?

Reflection

Jack and Nina really cared for each other: their care helped them both when they were poorly. It's easy to be kind and to help someone, so why not try it – there are so many ways to show that you care.

Prayer

Lord God, thank you that there are lots of people who take care of me. Please help me to be a caring person who thinks about others. Please help me to care for the people in my family by being kind and helpful. Help me to remember to say thank you for all the care I get. Amen.

4E BULLYING: WHAT IS BULLYING?

Objective

To help children understand what bullying is and how to respond to it.

PSHE/Citizenship links

4e: teasing and bullying.

Preparation

This assembly is a presentation in the form of a simple script, like a play script. It requires five children, A to E, to act out the five parts. They'll need to be good, confident readers with clear voices. You'll need to have a couple of practices with the children in the hall too. No props are needed.

Introduction

The assembly today is about bullying. Some people aren't really sure exactly what bullying is, so today's assembly will help you to tell when someone is being a bully and when someone isn't. The assembly is going to be performed by these five children.

DRAMA SCRIPT: WHAT IS BULLYING?

A What's the matter? You look sad.
B That new girl just called me a horrible name.
C You should tell the teacher – that's bullying.
D But if she did it just once it's not bullying.
E I thought that calling people bad names is bullying.
A It can be, but only if someone does it to the same person a lot.
B What do you mean?
C Please explain.
D Well, bullying is when someone keeps doing something bad to you.
E But name calling is bad.
A Yes, but it's not really bullying if someone just does it once.
B Well, the new girl just did it once.
C So maybe she isn't a bully.
D The best thing is to wait and see if she keeps doing it to you.
E So, when should we tell the teacher?
A Well, you can't tell the teacher about every little thing that happens.
B Yes, teachers are busy and they haven't got time for that.
C But they want to know if a really bad thing happens.
D Yes, if someone keeps calling you names then they want to know.
E What else do they want to know about?
A Teasing maybe?
B Yes, if someone keeps teasing you, that can be bullying.

C Nipping and hitting is bad too.
D Yes, you should tell the teacher about that.
E But you can't tell them about every little push that happens in the playground.
A What if you see someone else being hurt?
B Well, you should go over and be kind to the person who was hurt.
C But should you tell a teacher?
D It depends how bad it was.
E If the person who did it keeps doing it, then you should tell a teacher.
A Because that's bullying.
B Yes, it's picking on someone.
C And doing it again and again.
D It's hurting or upsetting someone a lot.
E We don't want bullying in this school, so let's all try to stop it.
All Right!

Interactive Follow-up

Questions

1. Was the new girl being a bully?
   (No, because she only called someone a name once.)
2. Name-calling can be bullying if what happens?
   (If someone keeps doing it to the same person lots of times, upsetting them.)
3. What should you do if you see someone being bullied? *(Tell a teacher.)*

Getting the message

Some things are bullying and some are not. Call out yes or no to these questions:

- If one person calls you a name once, is that bullying?
- If someone keeps calling someone else a bad name, is that bullying?
- Do bullies always tease people?
- Do bullies sometimes hurt people by things like hitting or kicking?
- Is a bully a person who picks on another person lots of times?
- Is it best to tell someone if you think you are being bullied?
- Should you tell your teacher every time you get a little bit upset?

NON-INTERACTIVE FOLLOW-UP

Summary

- Calling someone a name once is not bullying.
- Bullying is when someone upsets the same person lots of times.
- Teachers should be told if bullying goes on, but they should not be told about every little minor upset at school.
- Bullying can include teasing and physical actions.

Something to think about

Why do bullies bully people?

Reflection

Bullying is when one person hurts or upsets another person lots of times. It's a very bad thing, so if you are bullied or if you see someone else being bullied you must tell someone, even if you are frightened. By being brave you can stop bullying.

Prayer

Lord God, thank you that there are people we can turn to for help if we are being bullied. Please help bullies to stop what they are doing and treat people kindly. Help us not to use bad names or to tease and upset others. Help us to be brave to tell a grown up if we are being bullied or if we see someone else being bullied. Amen.

APPENDIX: SEAL LINKS

Assembly	SEAL link
1a Right and wrong	self awareness, motivation, social skills
1b Sharing opinions	self awareness, empathy, motivation
1c Feelings	self awareness, managing feelings, empathy
1d Recognising strengths	self awareness, managing feelings, motivation
1e Setting goals	self awareness, motivation
2a Taking part in discussions	managing feelings, motivation, empathy, social skills
2b Taking part in debate	self awareness, social skills
2c Recognising choices	self awareness, empathy, motivation, social skills
2d Following rules	self awareness, motivation, social skills
2e Meeting needs	self awareness, managing feelings, motivation, empathy, social skills
2f Belonging	self awareness, empathy, social skills
2g Improving the environment	motivation, social skills
2h Making a contribution	motivation, social skills
2i Where money comes from and goes to	self awareness, managing feelings, motivation
3a Improving health	self awareness, motivation
3b Personal hygiene	self awareness, motivation, social skills
3c How diseases spread	self awareness, motivation, empathy, social skills
3d Growing from young to old	self awareness, empathy, social skills
3f Household products	self awareness, managing feelings, motivation
3g Rules for keeping safe	self awareness, managing feelings, motivation, social skills
4a How our behaviour affects others	self awareness, managing feelings, empathy, social skills
4b Listening to others	self awareness, motivation, social skills
4c Respecting differences	self awareness, motivation, empathy, social skills
4d Caring for each other	self awareness, managing feelings, empathy
4e Bullying	self awareness, managing feelings, empathy, social skills

Badger Publishing Limited
15 Wedgwood Gate, Pin Green Industrial Estate,
Stevenage, Hertfordshire SG1 4SU
Telephone: 01438 356907
Fax: 01438 747015
www.badger-publishing.co.uk
enquiries@badger-publishing.co.uk

Badger Assembly Stories: Citizenship and PSHE volume 2
Ages 5-7
ISBN 978 1 84691 105 7

Publisher: David Jamieson
Editor: Paul Martin
Designer: Adam Wilmott

Printed in the UK.